OpenStack for Architects
Second Edition

Design production-ready private cloud infrastructure

Ben Silverman
Michael Solberg

BIRMINGHAM - MUMBAI

OpenStack for Architects
Second Edition

Commissioning Editor: Gebin George
Acquisition Editor: Meeta Rajani
Content Development Editor: Devika Battike
Technical Editor: Prachi Sawant
Copy Editors: Dipti Mankame, Safis Editing
Project Coordinator: Judie Jose
Proofreader: Safis Editing
Indexer: Mariammal Chettiyar
Graphics: Tom Scaria
Production Coordinator: Aparna Bhagat

First published: February 2017
Second edition: May 2018

Production reference: 1300518

Published by Packt Publishing Ltd.
Livery Place
35 Livery Street
Birmingham
B3 2PB, UK.

ISBN 978-1-78862-451-0

www.packtpub.com

`mapt.io`

Mapt is an online digital library that gives you full access to over 5,000 books and videos, as well as industry leading tools to help you plan your personal development and advance your career. For more information, please visit our website.

Why subscribe?

- Spend less time learning and more time coding with practical eBooks and Videos from over 4,000 industry professionals

- Improve your learning with Skill Plans built especially for you

- Get a free eBook or video every month

- Mapt is fully searchable

- Copy and paste, print, and bookmark content

PacktPub.com

Did you know that Packt offers eBook versions of every book published, with PDF and ePub files available? You can upgrade to the eBook version at `www.PacktPub.com` and as a print book customer, you are entitled to a discount on the eBook copy. Get in touch with us at `service@packtpub.com` for more details.

At `www.PacktPub.com`, you can also read a collection of free technical articles, sign up for a range of free newsletters, and receive exclusive discounts and offers on Packt books and eBooks.

Contributors

About the authors

Ben Silverman, the Chief Cloud Officer for the service provider/Telco team at OnX. Previously, Ben has worked as a Sr. system architect for Mirantis and as the lead architect for American Express's first OpenStack cloud. He is also responsible for the OpenStack Architecture Guide online and leads the Phoenix OpenStack User's group. He holds a degree in English communications and a master's degree in information management from Arizona State University.

He has also been a technical reviewer of the book, *Learning OpenStack*, by Packt Publishing.

> *I'd like to thank God for the blessings that have allowed me to write this book. I'd also like to thank my beautiful wife Jennifer and the two apples of my eyes, my sons, Jason and Brayden, for all of the loving support. I'd also like to thank all the stackers that continue to give us feedback and help us write better books.*

Michael Solberg, as a chief architect, is responsible for helping Red Hat customers achieve their key business transformation initiatives through open source architectures and technologies. His previous experience includes building web hosting infrastructure, helping enterprises migrate to Linux, and designing new Infrastructure-as-a-Service platforms. He is an avid supporter of the OpenStack project and a regular speaker at industry events.

> *Thanks to Ben for all of his hard work on this edition of the book. It's a great pleasure to work with such a talented author.*

About the reviewer

Felipe Monteiro currently works for AT&T as a software developer, predominantly focusing on developing AT&T's under-cloud platform in order to orchestrate OpenStack on Kubernetes deployment. He is currently the lead developer for Deckhand and Armada, two of the core microservices that comprise UCP. He also works on OpenStack, particularly on Murano, OpenStack's application catalog, and Patrole, a Tempest plugin. He was the Murano PTL during the Pike release cycle, and he is currently a core reviewer for both Murano and Patrole.

Packt is searching for authors like you

If you're interested in becoming an author for Packt, please visit authors.packtpub.com and apply today. We have worked with thousands of developers and tech professionals, just like you, to help them share their insight with the global tech community. You can make a general application, apply for a specific hot topic that we are recruiting an author for, or submit your own idea.

Table of Contents

Preface

Over the past 6 years, hundreds of organizations have successfully implemented Infrastructure as a Service (IaaS) platforms based on OpenStack. The huge amount of investment from these organizations, industry giants, such as IBM, Cisco, Intel and HP, as well as open source leaders, such as Red Hat, Canonical, and SUSE, have led analysts to label OpenStack as the most important open source technology since the Linux operating system. Due to its ambitious scope, OpenStack is a complex and fast-evolving open source project that requires a diverse skill set to design and implement it.

This guide leads you through the major decision points that you'll face while architecting an OpenStack private cloud for your organization. This book will address the latest changes made in the latest OpenStack release and will also deal with advanced concepts, such as containerization, NVF, and security. At each point, we offer you advice based on the experience we've gained from designing and leading successful OpenStack projects in a wide range of industries. Each chapter also includes lab material that gives you a chance to install and configure the technologies used to build production-quality OpenStack clouds. Most importantly, we focus on ensuring that your OpenStack project meets the needs of your organization, which will guarantee a successful rollout.

Who this book is for

If you are a cloud architect who is responsible for designing and implementing private cloud with OpenStack, then this book is for you. System engineers and Enterprise architects will also find this book useful. Basic understanding of core OpenStack services as well as some working experience of concepts is recommended.

What this book covers

Chapter 1, *Introduction to OpenStack*, provides an overview of the OpenStack project. It covers the history, goals, governance, and components of the software. It also provides some examples of how the software has been used successfully in different industries to entice the reader to follow through the rest of the book. Finally, it provides the reader with an initial plan for architecting an OpenStack cloud.

Chapter 2, *Architecting the Cloud,* walks the reader through the initial set of choices that an organization makes when first designing their OpenStack cloud. Options are presented with guidance for software, hardware, network, and storage selection. In addition, physical site placement is discussed.

Chapter 3, *Planning for Failure,* covers design decisions that impact the scalability and availability of the cloud.

Chapter 4, *Building the Deployment Pipeline,* introduces the tenants of DevOps and translates them into a continuously integrated and delivered OpenStack deployment. The available configuration management system options for OpenStack are discussed, and the tools for driving automated builds are described.

Chapter 5, *Building to Operate,* covers day 2 management of OpenStack clouds and how architects can simplify operations through planning. Various tools and methods for monitoring, orchestration, and analytics are introduced.

Chapter 6, *Integrating the Platform,* describes the various integration strategies available for OpenStack clouds. Topics ranging from active directory integration to SOA Governance and API contracts are covered.

Chapter 7, *Securing the Cloud,* covers design considerations for the virtual environment inside of the OpenStack cloud.

Chapter 8, *OpenStack Use Cases,* walks the reader through some of the most popular use cases for OpenStack. Physical and virtual considerations for each use case and sample configurations are given.

Chapter 9, *Containers,* shows that the adoption of containers is dramatically changing the way we deploy and use OpenStack today. This chapter explores how to best use them to improve deployments.

Chapter 10, *Conclusion,* provides some forward-looking guidance on emerging technologies in the OpenStack space and how to integrate them into the deployment from earlier in the book.

To get the most out of this book

All the software used in the examples in this book is available at no cost on the internet. Links are provided for each of the projects used. Many of the lab exercises require access to physical hardware or a virtualized environment for a lab. We recommend having at least 4 and up to 12 physical servers available for deploying OpenStack into production, depending on your requirements.

Download the example code files

You can download the example code files for this book from your account at www.packtpub.com. If you purchased this book elsewhere, you can visit www.packtpub.com/support and register to have the files emailed directly to you.

You can download the code files by following these steps:

1. Log in or register at www.packtpub.com.
2. Select the **SUPPORT** tab.
3. Click on **Code Downloads & Errata**.
4. Enter the name of the book in the **Search** box and follow the onscreen instructions.

Once the file is downloaded, please make sure that you unzip or extract the folder using the latest version of:

- WinRAR/7-Zip for Windows
- Zipeg/iZip/UnRarX for Mac
- 7-Zip/PeaZip for Linux

The code bundle for the book is also hosted on GitHub at https://github.com/PacktPublishing/OpenStack-for-Architects-Second-Edition. In case there's an update to the code, it will be updated on the existing GitHub repository.

We also have other code bundles from our rich catalog of books and videos available at https://github.com/PacktPublishing/. Check them out!

Download the color images

We also provide a PDF file that has color images of the screenshots/diagrams used in this book. You can download it from `https://www.packtpub.com/sites/default/files/downloads/OpenStackforArchitectsSecondEdition_ColorImages.pdf`.

Conventions used

There are a number of text conventions used throughout this book.

`CodeInText`: Indicates code words in text, database table names, folder names, filenames, file extensions, pathnames, dummy URLs, user input, and Twitter handles. Here is an example: "Copy the `/etc/glance` and `/var/lib/glance` directories."

A block of code is set as follows:

```
listen_tls = 1
listen_tcp = 0
auth_tls = "none"
```

Any command-line input or output is written as follows:

```
# packstack --allinone
```

Bold: Indicates a new term, an important word, or words that you see onscreen. For example, words in menus or dialog boxes appear in the text like this. Here is an example: "Under **Build**, click on **Add build step** and select **Execute shell**."

Warnings or important notes appear like this.

Tips and tricks appear like this.

Get in touch

Feedback from our readers is always welcome.

General feedback: Email `feedback@packtpub.com` and mention the book title in the subject of your message. If you have questions about any aspect of this book, please email us at `questions@packtpub.com`.

Errata: Although we have taken every care to ensure the accuracy of our content, mistakes do happen. If you have found a mistake in this book, we would be grateful if you would report this to us. Please visit `www.packtpub.com/submit-errata`, selecting your book, clicking on the Errata Submission Form link, and entering the details.

Piracy: If you come across any illegal copies of our works in any form on the Internet, we would be grateful if you would provide us with the location address or website name. Please contact us at `copyright@packtpub.com` with a link to the material.

If you are interested in becoming an author: If there is a topic that you have expertise in and you are interested in either writing or contributing to a book, please visit `authors.packtpub.com`.

Reviews

Please leave a review. Once you have read and used this book, why not leave a review on the site that you purchased it from? Potential readers can then see and use your unbiased opinion to make purchase decisions, we at Packt can understand what you think about our products, and our authors can see your feedback on their book. Thank you!

For more information about Packt, please visit `packtpub.com`.

Introducing OpenStack 1

At the Vancouver OpenStack Conference in May 2015, US retail giant Walmart announced that they had deployed an OpenStack cloud with 140,000 cores of compute, supporting 1.5 billion page views on Cyber Monday. CERN, a long-time OpenStack user, announced that their OpenStack private cloud had grown to 100,000 cores, running computational workloads on two petabytes of disk in production. In the years since then, telecommunications giants across the globe, including AT&T, Verizon, and NTT, have all begun the process of moving the backbone of the internet from purpose-built hardware onto virtualized network functions running on OpenStack.

The scale of the OpenStack project and its deployment is staggering—a given semi-annual release of the OpenStack software contains tens of thousands of commits from hundreds of developers from dozens of companies.

In this chapter, we'll look at what OpenStack is and why it has been so influential. We'll also take the first steps in architecting a cloud.

What is OpenStack?

OpenStack is best defined by its use cases, as users and contributors approach the software with many different goals in mind. For hosting providers such as Rackspace, OpenStack provides the infrastructure for a multitenant shared services platform. For others, it might provide a mechanism for provisioning data and compute for a distributed business intelligence application. There are a few answers to this question that are relevant, regardless of your organization's use case.

OpenStack – an API

One of the initial goals of OpenStack was to provide **Application Program Interface** (**API**) compatibility with the Amazon Web Service. As the popularity of the platform has increased, the OpenStack API has become a de facto standard on its own. In the November 2017 User Survey, the standard APIs were listed as the number one business driver for the adoption of OpenStack as a private cloud platform. As such, many of the enterprise organizations that we've worked with to create OpenStack clouds are using them as an underlying **Infrastructure as a Service** (**IaaS**) layer for one or more **Platform as a Service** (**PaaS**) or Hybrid Cloud deployments.

Every feature or function of OpenStack is exposed in one of its REST APIs. There are command-line interfaces for OpenStack (legacy `nova` and the newer `openstack` common client) as well as a standard web interface (Horizon). However, most interactions between the components and end users happen over the API. This is advantageous for the following reasons:

- Everything in the system can be automated
- Integration with other systems is well-defined
- Use cases can be clearly defined and automatically tested

 The APIs are well-defined and versioned REST APIs, and there are native clients and SDKs for more than a dozen programming languages. For a full list of current SDKs, refer to: `http://api.openstack.org`.

OpenStack – an open source software project

OpenStack is an open source software project which has a huge number of contributors from a wide range of organizations. OpenStack was originally created by NASA and Rackspace. Rackspace is still a significant contributor to OpenStack, but these days, contributions to the project comes from a wide array of companies, including the traditional open source contributors (Red Hat, IBM, and HP) as well as companies that are dedicated entirely to OpenStack (Mirantis and CloudBase). Contributions come in the form of drivers for particular pieces of infrastructure (that is, Cinder block storage drivers or Neutron SDN drivers), bug fixes, or new features in the core projects.

OpenStack is governed by a foundation. Membership in the foundation is free and open to anyone who wishes to join. There are currently thousands of members in the foundation. Leadership on technical issues is provided by a 13-member technical committee, which is generally elected by the individual members. Strategic and financial issues are decided by a board of directors, which include members appointed by corporate sponsors and elected by the individual members.

 For more information on joining or contributing to the OpenStack Foundation, refer to: http://www.openstack.org/foundation.

OpenStack is written in the Python programming language and is usually deployed on the Linux operating system. The source code is readily available on the internet and commits are welcome from the community at large. Before code is committed to the project, it has to pass through a series of gates, which includes unit testing and code review.

OpenStack – a private cloud platform

Finally, OpenStack provides the software modules necessary to build an automated private cloud platform. Although OpenStack has traditionally been focused on providing IaaS capabilities in the style of Amazon Web Services, new projects have been introduced lately, which begin to provide capabilities that might be associated more with Platform as a Service. This book will focus on implementing the core set of OpenStack components described as follows.

The most important aspect of OpenStack pertaining to its usage as a private cloud platform is the tenant model. The authentication and authorization services that provide this model are implemented in the identity service, Keystone. Every virtual or physical object governed by the OpenStack system exists within a private space referred to as a **tenant** or **project**. The latest version of the Keystone API has differentiated itself further to include a higher level construct named a **domain**. Regardless of the terminology, the innate ability to securely segregate compute, network, and storage resources is the most fundamental capability of the platform. This is what differentiates it from traditional data center virtualization and makes it a private cloud platform.

OpenStack components

OpenStack is a modular system. Although some OpenStack Architects choose to implement a reference architecture of all of the core components shipped by an OpenStack distributor, many will only implement the services required to meet their business cases.

Reference implementations are typically used for development use cases where the final production state of the service might not be well-defined. Production deployments will likely gate the availability of some services to reduce the amount of configuration and testing required for implementation. Reference deployments will typically not vary from the distributor's implementation so that the distributor's deployment and testing tools can be reused without modification.

In this book, we'll be focusing on the following core components of OpenStack.

Compute

OpenStack Compute (Nova) is one of the original components of OpenStack. It provides the ability to provision a virtual machine, an application container, or a physical system, depending on configuration. All provisioning is image-based, and the OpenStack Image Service (Glance) is a prerequisite for the Compute service. Some kind of networking is also required to launch a compute instance.

Networking was originally provided by the Compute service in OpenStack, but the use of Nova Networking was deprecated in the Newton release of OpenStack, and it is no longer supported. Networking is provided by the Neutron service, which offers a wide range of functionality.

In OpenStack, we refer to provisioned compute nodes as **instances** and not **virtual machines**. Although this might seem like a matter of semantics, it's a useful device for a few reasons. The first reason is that it describes the deployment mechanism; all compute in OpenStack is the instantiation of a Glance image with a specified hardware template, the **flavor**.

The flavor describes the characteristics of the instantiated image, and it normally represents a number of cores of compute with a given amount of memory and storage. Storage may be provided by the Compute service or the block storage service, Cinder. Although quotas are defined to limit the amount of cores, memory, and storage available to a given user (the tenant), charge-back is traditionally established by the flavor (that is, instantiating a particular image on an m1-small flavor may cost a tenant a certain number of cents an hour).

The second reason that the term instance is useful is that virtual machines in OpenStack do not typically have the same life cycle as they do in traditional virtualization. Although we might expect virtual machines to have a multiyear life cycle like physical machines, we would expect instances to have a life cycle which is measured in days or weeks. Virtual machines are backed up and recovered, whereas instances are rescued or evacuated. Legacy virtualization platforms assume resizing and modifying behaviors are in place; cloud platforms such as OpenStack expect redeployment of virtual machines or adding additional capacity through additional instances, not adding additional resources to existing virtual machines.

The third reason that we find it useful to use the term instance is that the Compute service has evolved over the years to launch a number of different types of compute. Some OpenStack deployments may only launch physical machines, whereas others may launch a combination of physical, virtual, and container-based instances. The same construct applies, regardless of the compute provider.

Some of the lines between virtual machines and instances are becoming more blurred as more enterprise features are added to the OpenStack Compute service. Later on, we'll discuss some of the ways in which we can launch instances which act more like virtual machines for more traditional compute workloads.

Object storage

Ephemeral backing storage for compute instances is provided by the Nova service. This storage is referred to as **ephemeral** because its life cycle coterminates with the life cycle of the compute instance. That is, when an instance is terminated, the ephemeral storage associated with the instance is deleted from the compute host on which it resided. The first kind of persistent storage provided in the OpenStack system was object storage, based on the S3 service available in the Amazon Web Service environment.

Object Storage is provided by the Swift service in OpenStack. Just as Nova provides an EC2- compatible compute API, Swift provides an S3-compatible object storage API. Applications which are written to run on the Amazon EC2 service and read and write their persistent data to the S3 Object Storage service do not need to be rewritten to run on an OpenStack system.

A number of third-party applications provide an S3 or Swift-compatible API, and they may be substituted for Swift in a typical OpenStack deployment. These include open source object stores, such as Gluster or Ceph, or proprietary ones, such as Scality or Cloudian. The Swift service is broken down into a few components, and third-party applications may use the *Proxy* component of Swift for API services and implement only a backend, or may replace the Swift service entirely. All OpenStack-compatible object stores will consume the tenant model of OpenStack and accept Keystone tokens for authentication.

Block storage

Traditional persistent storage is provided to OpenStack workloads through the Cinder block storage component. The life cycle of Cinder volumes is maintained independent of compute instances, and volumes may be attached or detached to one or more compute instances to provide a backing store for filesystem-based storage.

OpenStack ships with a reference implementation of Cinder, which leverages local storage on the host and uses LVM as well as the ability to use iSCSI to share a block device attached to a Cinder **storage node** that can use its storage for instances. This implementation lacks high availability, and it is typically only used in test environments. Production deployments tend to leverage a software-based or hardware-based block storage solution, such as Ceph or NetApp, chosen based on performance and availability requirements.

Network

The last of the foundational services in OpenStack is Neutron, the Network service. Neutron provides an API for creating ports, subnets, networks, and routers. Additional network services, such as firewalls and load balancers, are provided in some OpenStack deployments.

As with Cinder, the reference implementation, based on Open vSwitch, is typically used in test environments or smaller deployments. Large-scale production deployments will leverage one of the many available software-based or hardware-based SDN solutions, which have Neutron drivers. These solutions range from open source implementations such as Juniper's OpenContrail to proprietary solutions such as VMware's NSX platform.

Common OpenStack use cases

In spite of immense interest, huge investment, and public success, we've seen a number of cases where well-intentioned OpenStack projects fail or are at least perceived as a failure by the people who have funded them. When OpenStack projects fail, the technology itself is rarely the root cause. Thomas Bittman at Gartner noticed this trend and wrote an influential blog post entitled *Why are Private Clouds Failing?* in September 2014.

Bittman's findings echo many of our experiences from the field. In short, the reason that most private cloud projects fail is that improper expectations were set from the beginning, and the business goals for the cloud weren't realized by the end result.

First and foremost, OpenStack deployments should be seen as an investment with returns and not a project to reduce operational costs. Although we've certainly seen dramatic reductions in operational workloads through the automation that OpenStack provides, it is difficult to accurately quantify those reductions in order to justify the operational investment required to run an efficient cloud platform. Organizations that are entirely focused on cutting costs through automation should first look at automating existing virtual environments instead of deploying new environments.

We've also seen a lot of projects that had poorly quantified goals. OpenStack is an enabler of use cases and not an IT panacea. If the use cases are not agreed upon before investment in the platform begins, it will prove very difficult to justify the investment in the end. This is why the role of the Architect is so critical in OpenStack deployments—it is their job to ensure that concrete requirements are written upfront so that all of the stakeholders can quantify the success of the platform once deployed.

With this in mind, let's take a look at some typical use cases for OpenStack deployments.

Public hosting

As we mentioned before, OpenStack was originally created with code contributions from NASA and Rackspace. NASA's interest in OpenStack sprang from their desire to create a private elastic compute cloud, whereas the primary goal for Rackspace was to create an open source platform that could replace their public shared hosting infrastructure. As of April 2015, the *Rackspace Public Cloud* offering had been ported to OpenStack and had passed the **OpenStack Powered Platform** certification.

The Rackspace implementation offers both Compute and Object Storage services, but some implementations may choose to offer only Compute or Object Storage and receive certifications for those services. DreamHost, another public OpenStack-based cloud provider, for example, has chosen to break their managed services down into **DreamCompute** and **DreamObjects**, which implement the services separately. The DreamObjects service was implemented and offered first as a compliment to DreamHost's existing shared web hosting, and the DreamCompute service was introduced later.

Most public hosting providers focus primarily on the Compute service, and many do not yet offer software-defined networking through the Neutron network service (DreamCompute being a notable exception). Architects of hosting platforms will focus first on tenancy issues, second on chargeback issues, and finally on scale.

High-performance computing

The first production deployment of OpenStack outside NASA and Rackspace was at a Canadian not-for-profit organization named Cybera. Cybera deployed OpenStack as a technology platform in 2011 for its DAIR program, which provides free compute and storage to Canadian researchers, entrepreneurs, and small businesses.

Architects at Cybera, NASA, and CERN have all commented on how their services have much of the same concerns as in the public hosting space. They provide compute and storage resources to researchers and don't have much insight into how those resources will actually be used. Thus, concerns about secure multitenancy will apply to these environments just as much as they do in the hosting space.

HPC clouds will have an added focus on performance, though. Although hosting providers will look to economize on commodity hardware, research clouds will look to maximize performance by configuring their compute, storage, and network hardware to support high volume and throughput operations. Where most clouds will work best by growing low-to-mid range hardware horizontally with commodity hardware, high-performance clouds tend to be very specific about the performance profiles of their hardware selection. Cybera has published performance benchmarks, comparing its DAIR platform to EC2. Architects of research clouds may also look to use hardware pass-through capabilities or other low-level hypervisor features to enable specific workloads.

Rapid application development

Over the past couple of years, a third significant use case has emerged for OpenStack—enterprise application development environments. While public hosting and high-performance compute implementations may have huge regions with hundreds of compute nodes and thousands of cores, enterprise implementations tend to have regions of 20 to 50 compute nodes. Enterprise adopters have a strong interest in software-defined networking.

The primary driver for enterprise adoption of OpenStack has been the increasing use of continuous integration and continuous delivery in the application development workflow. A typical **Continuous Integration and Continuous Delivery (CI/CD)** workflow will deploy a complete application on every developer commit, which passes basic unit tests in order to perform automated integration testing. These application deployments live as long as it takes to run the unit tests, and then an automated process tears down the deployment once the tests pass or fail. This workflow is easily facilitated with a combination of OpenStack compute and network services.

While Architects of hosting or **High-Performance Computing (HPC)** clouds spend a lot of time focusing on tenancy and scaling issues, Architects of enterprise deployments will spend a lot of time focusing on how to integrate OpenStack compute into their existing infrastructure. Enterprise deployments will frequently leverage existing service catalog implementations and identity management solutions. Many enterprise deployments will also need to integrate with existing IPAM and asset tracking systems.

Network Function Virtualization

One of the largest areas for development and deployment of the OpenStack platform has been in the telecommunications industry. **Network Functions Virtualization (NFV)** provides a common IaaS platform for that industry, which is in the process of replacing the purpose-built hardware devices that provide network services with virtualized appliances that run on commodity hardware. Some of these services are routing, proxies, content filtering, as well as packet core services and high-volume switching. Most of these appliances have intense compute requirements, and they are largely stateless. These workloads are well-suited for the OpenStack compute model.

NFV use cases typically leverage hardware features, which can directly attach compute instances to physical network interfaces on compute nodes. Instances are also typically very sensitive to CPU, and memory topology (NUMA) and virtual cores tend to be mapped directly to physical cores. Orchestration either through Heat or TOSCA has also been a large focus for these deployments.

Architects of NFV solutions will focus primarily on virtual instance placement and performance issues and less on tenancy and integration issues.

Drafting an initial deployment plan

OpenStack is designed to be used at scale. Many IT projects might comprise a few physical assets deployed within an existing network, storage, and compute landscape, but OpenStack deployments are, by definition, new network, storage, and compute landscapes. Any project of this size and scope requires significant coordination between different teams within an IT organization. This kind of coordination requires careful planning and, in our experience, a lot of documentation.

The role of the Architect

This book is written to provide best practices for a relatively new role within many organizations—the Cloud Architect. The Cloud Architect's primary function is to take business requirements for Infrastructure or Platform as a Service and design an Infrastructure or Platform as a Service solution, which meets those requirements. This requires an in-depth knowledge of the capabilities of the infrastructure software paired with competency in network and storage architecture.

The typical Cloud Architect will have a background in compute and will lean heavily on the Network and Storage Architects within an organization to round out their technical knowledge. Since OpenStack is based on the Linux operating system, most OpenStack Architects will have a deep knowledge of that platform. But as we mentioned earlier, OpenStack is typically delivered as an API, and OpenStack Architects will need to have fluency in application development as well.

OpenStack Architects are responsible first and foremost for authoring and maintaining a set of design and deployment documentation. It's difficult to describe an ocean if you've never seen one, so this book will walk you through implementation of the documentation that you will create as you create it.

The design document

The first document that we will create is the design document. This may be named something different in your organization, but the goal of the design document is to explain the reasoning behind all of the choices that were made in the implementation of the platform. The format may vary from team to team, but we want to capture the following points:

- **Background**: This is the history behind the decision to start the project. If the document will only be consumed internally, this can be pretty short. If it's going to be consumed externally, this is an opportunity to provide organizational context for your vendors and partners.
- **Summary**: This is really just a detailed summary of the entire document. Typically, this part of the deliverable will be used by managers, technology, and business leaders to understand the business impact of the overall recommendation. Requirements and the resulting architecture should be summarized.
- **Requirements**: This is the meat of the document. Requirements can be in whatever format is acceptable for your project management team. We prefer the *user story* format and will use that in the examples in this book.
- **Physical architecture**: This is an explanation of roles and physical machines that take those roles. This should include a network diagram.
- **Service architecture**: This is a summary of available services and their relationships. This section should include a service diagram.
- **Tenant architecture**: A section should be included that describes the expected landscape inside the cloud. This includes things such as available compute flavors, images, identity management architecture, and IPAM or DDI.
- **Roadmap**: This section is optional and often lives in another document. It's an opportunity to identify areas for improvement in future releases of the platform.

The design document often goes through a number of revisions as the project is developed. An important step at the end of each iteration of the platform is to reconcile any changes made to the platform with the design document.

 Beware of scope creep in the design document. This artifact has a tendency to turn into documentation on how OpenStack works. Remember to focus on explaining the decisions you made instead of what all the available options at the time were.

The deployment plan

Every implementation of OpenStack should start with a deployment plan. The design document describes what's being deployed and why, whereas the deployment plan describes how. Like the design document, the content of a deployment plan varies from organization to organization. It should at least include the following things:

- **Hardware**: This is a list of the compute, storage, and network hardware available for the deployment.
- **Network addressing**: This is a table of IP and MAC addresses for the network assets in the deployment. For deployments of hundreds of compute nodes, this should probably be limited to a set of VLANs and subnets available for the deployment.
- **Deployment-specific configuration**: We'll assume that the configuration of the OpenStack deployment is automated. These are any settings that an engineer would need to adjust before launching the automated deployment of the environment.
- **Requirements**: These are things that need to be in place before the deployment can proceed. Normally, this is hardware configuration, switch configuration, LUN masking, and so on.

A good deployment plan will document everything that an engineering team needs to know to take the design document and instantiate it in the physical world. One thing that we like to leave out of the deployment plan is step-by-step instructions on how to deploy OpenStack. That information typically lives in an Installation Guide, which may be provided by a vendor or written by the operations team.

Your first OpenStack deployment

In our experience, almost all organizations approach OpenStack with the following three steps:

1. An individual, usually a Linux or Cloud Architect, installs OpenStack on a single machine to verify that the software can be deployed without too much effort.
2. The Architect enlists the help of other team members, typically Network and Storage Architects or Engineers to deploy a multiple-node installation. This will leverage some kind of shared ephemeral or block storage.

3. A team of Architects or Engineers craft the first deployment of OpenStack, which is customized for the organization's use cases or environmental concerns. Professional services from a company, such as Red Hat, Mirantis, HP, IBM, Canonical, or Rackspace, are often engaged at this point in the process.

From here on out, it's off to the races. We'll follow a similar pattern in this book. In this first chapter, we'll start with the first step—the *all-in-one* deployment.

Writing the initial deployment plan

Taking the time to document the very first deployment might seem a bit obsessive, but it provides us with the opportunity to begin iterating on the documentation that is the key to successful OpenStack deployments. We'll start with the following template.

Hardware

The initial deployment of OpenStack will leverage a single commodity server, a HP DL380. Its details are listed in the following table:

Hostname	Model	CPU cores	Memory	Disk	Network
openstack	DL380	16	256 GB	500 GB	2 x 10 GB

This deployment provides a compute capacity for 60 m1.medium instances or 30 m1.large instances.

Change the specifications in the table to meet your deployment. It's important to specify the expected capacity in the deployment document. For a basic rule of thumb, just divide the amount of available system memory by the instance memory. We'll talk more about accurately forecasting capacity in a later chapter.

Network addressing

There is one physical provider network in this deployment. SDN is provided in the tenant space by Neutron with the OVS ML2 plugin. Its details are listed in the following table:

Hostname	MAC	IP
openstack	3C:97:0E:BF:6C:78	192.168.0.10

Change the network addresses in this section to meet your deployment. We'll only use a single network interface for the all-in-one installation.

Configuration notes

This deployment will use the RDO all-in-one reference architecture. This reference architecture uses a minimum amount of hardware as the basis for a monolithic installation of OpenStack, typically only used for testing or experimentation. For more information on the all-in-one deployment, refer to: https://www.rdoproject.org/.

For the first deployment, we'll just use the RDO distribution of the box. In later chapters, we'll begin to customize our deployment and add notes to this section to describe where we've diverged from the reference architecture.

Requirements

The host system will need to meet the following requirements prior to deployment:

- Red Hat Enterprise Linux 7 (or CentOS 7)
- Network Manager must be disabled
- Network interfaces must be configured as per the *Network Addressing* section in /etc/sysconfig/network-scripts
- The RDO OpenStack repository must be enabled (from: https://rdoproject.org/)

To enable the RDO repository, run the following command as the **root** user on your system:

```
# yum install -y https://rdoproject.org/repos/rdo-release.rpm
```

Installing OpenStack

Assuming that we've correctly configured our host machine as per our deployment plan, the actual deployment of OpenStack is relatively straightforward. The installation instructions can either be captured in an additional section of the deployment plan, or they can be captured in a separate document—the Installation Guide. Either way, the installation instructions should be immediately followed by a set of tests that can be run to verify that the deployment went correctly.

Installation instructions

To install OpenStack, execute the following command as the **root** user on the system designated in the deployment plan:

```
# yum install -y openstack-packstack
```

This command will install the packstack installation utility on the machine. If this command fails, ensure that the RDO repository is correctly enabled using the following command:

```
# rpm -q rdo-release
```

If the RDO repository has not been enabled, enable it using the following command:

```
# yum install -y https://rdoproject.org/repos/rdo-release.rpm
```

Next, run the packstack utility to install OpenStack:

```
# packstack --allinone
```

The packstack utility configures and applies a set of puppet manifests to your system to install and configure the OpenStack distribution. The --allinone option instructs packstack to configure the set of services defined in the reference architecture for RDO.

Verifying the installation

Once the installation has completed successfully, use the following steps to verify the installation.

First, verify the Keystone identity service by attempting to get an authorization token. The OpenStack command-line client uses a set of environment variables to authenticate your session. Two configuration files that set those variables will be created by the `packstack` installation utility.

The `keystonerc_admin` file can be used to authenticate an administrative user, and the `keystonerc_demo` file can be used to authenticate a nonprivileged user. An example `keystonerc` is shown as follows:

```
export OS_USERNAME=demo export OS_TENANT_NAME=demo
export OS_PASSWORD=<random string>
export OS_AUTH_URL=http://192.168.0.10:5000/v2.0/
export PS1='[\u@\h \W(keystone_demo)]\$ '
```

This file will be used to populate your command-line session with the necessary environment variables and credentials that will allow you to communicate with the OpenStack APIs that use the Keystone service for authentication.

In order to use the `keystonerc` file to load your credentials, source the contents into your shell session from the directory you ran the `packstack` command from. It will provide no output except for a shell prompt change:

```
# . ./keystonerc_demo
```

Your command prompt will change to remind you that you're using the sourced OpenStack credentials.

In order to load these credentials, the preceding source command must be run every time a user logs in. These credentials are not persistent. If you do not source your credentials before running OpenStack commands, you will most likely get the following error:

```
You must provide a username through either --os-username or
env[OS_USERNAME].
```

To verify the Keystone service, run the following command to get a Keystone token:

```
# openstack token issue
```

The output of this command should be a table similar to the following one:

```
+-----------+------------------------------------+
|  Property |  Value                             |
+-----------+------------------------------------+
|  expires  |  2015-07-14T05:01:41Z              |
|  id       |  a20264cd091847ac965cde8cbba7b0b9  |
|  tenant_id|  202bd2fa2a3a40639bb0bccc9a57e37d   |
|  user_id  |  68d90544e0064c4c838d47d80811b895   |
+-----------+------------------------------------+
```

Next, verify the Glance image service:

```
# openstack image list
```

This should output a table listing a single image, the CirrOS image that is installed with the `packstack` command. We'll use the ID of that glance image to verify the Nova Compute service. Before we do it, we'll verify the Neutron Network service:

```
# openstack network list
```

This should output a table listing a network available to use for testing. We'll use the ID of that network to verify the Nova Compute service with the following commands:

First, add the root's SSH key to OpenStack as demo.key:

```
# openstack keypair create --public-key ~/.ssh/id_rsa.pub demo
```

Now, create an instance named instance01:

```
# openstack server create --flavor m1.tiny \
--image <image_id> \
--key-name demo \
--nic net-id=<networkid> \
instance01
```

This command will create the instance and output a table of information about the instance that you've just created. To check the status of the instance as it is provisioned, use the following command:

```
# openstack server show instance01
```

When the status becomes ACTIVE, the instance has successfully launched. The key created with the nova keypair-add command (demo.key) can be used to log in to the instance once it's running.

Next steps

At this point, you should have a working OpenStack installation on a single machine. To familiarize yourself with the OpenStack Horizon user interface, see the documentation on the OpenStack website at `https://docs.openstack.org/nova/queens/user/launch-instances.html`.

Summary

This chapter provided background information on OpenStack and the component services that make up an OpenStack deployment. We looked at some typical use cases for OpenStack and discussed the role of the Cloud Architect in an organization that is embarking on an OpenStack private cloud deployment.

We also began the documentation for our OpenStack deployments. The documents such as the deployment plan and installation guide were created.

Finally, we completed an all-in-one OpenStack installation on a single server and verified the core set of services. This installation can be used to familiarize yourself with the OpenStack system. In the next chapter, we'll break down the different areas of design for OpenStack clouds and expand our documentation and deployment.

Further reading

Please refer to the following links for further reading:

- `https://www.openstack.org/summit/vancouver-2015/summit-videos/presentation/walmart-and-039s-cloud-journey`
- `https://www.openstack.org/videos/vancouver-2015/ceph-at-cern-a-year-in-the-life-of-a-petabyte-scale-block-storage-service`
- `https://www.openstack.org/user-stories/`
- `https://www.openstack.org/surveys/landing`
- `http://blogs.gartner.com/thomas_bittman/2014/09/12/why-are-private-clouds-failing`

- https://www.openstack.org/marketplace/public-clouds/rackspace/
  rackspace-public-cloud
- http://www.cybera.ca
- http://superuser.openstack.org/articles/openstack-users-share-how-
  their-deployments-stack-up

2
Architecting the Cloud

The array of possible hardware and software combinations that can be used to create an OpenStack cloud is pretty amazing at this point. A phrase we typically hear these days is that having an integration for OpenStack is *table stakes* for a hardware or software product coming in the market. As of the Queens release of OpenStack (March 2018), there were 75 Cinder storage drivers and over 40 Neutron network plugins. These integrations cover a wide range of products from traditional EMC storage arrays and Cisco switches to various software-defined storage and networking products. OpenStack supports a number of hypervisors and compute platforms, ranging from commodity x86 hardware to IBM Z-series mainframes.

A few of the decisions we make as architects affect the bottom line as much as hardware and software selection. Although we approach the deployment of our cloud or the development of our software in an iterative fashion to reduce the risk of mistakes, it is typically very difficult to iteratively purchase hardware.

Luckily, OpenStack ships with a set of **reference** plugins for each of the subsystems that we can use to mock out our cloud before purchasing actual hardware. For Cinder, the reference implementation involves using LVM and iSCSI on a Linux system. For Neutron, the reference implementation uses Open vSwitch and iptables on a Linux system. Even Compute can be mocked out using nested virtualization with KVM. The approach that we recommend is to begin an OpenStack project with the reference plugins until you get a feel of how the software and hardware will work together before making any large hardware or software purchases.

In this chapter, we will cover the following topics:

- Picking an OpenStack distribution
- Computing hardware considerations
- Network design
- Storage design
- Expanding the initial deployment

Picking an OpenStack distribution

OpenStack is developed like most open source software projects. The code is available at `http://openstack.org`, and it can be downloaded in the package format from: `http://tarballs.openstack.org`. As of the Queens release of OpenStack, there were over 700 individual projects available for download. That's a huge number of source repositories for an engineering team to sort through and manage, hence the development of the OpenStack distributions. Most of the OpenStack distributions are put together by the same groups that put together Linux distributions. For example, the three major distributions available are part of the Ubuntu, openSUSE, and CentOS Linux distributions. Each of these distributions maintain installation guides, which are available at: `http://docs.openstack.org`. There are also distributions available from companies, such as Suse, Mirantis, and Red Hat, which are part of commercial support agreements. These distributions are certified by the OpenStack Foundation, and a full list of them is available at: `https://www.openstack.org/marketplace/distros/`. In addition to these options, there are also companies such as Rackspace, which provide managed OpenStack deployments.

Running from the trunk

As we mentioned before, stable releases of OpenStack happen on a 6-month cadence. Active development happens in the trunk of each of the software projects (the *master* branch on the web-based repository service for OpenStack at: `http://git.openstack.org`). This master repository controls the distributed version control for the OpenStack project and aids in source code management. This is very similar to the well-known GitHub service used by many other open source projects. In addition to the Git repository, there are some number of stable branches corresponding to the 6-month releases. Features are implemented in the master branch, and bug fixes are backported from the trunk to the branches on an irregular basis.

For most organizations, taking a packaged version of one of the stable branches and deploying it will suffice. There are a couple of reasons why this might not be appealing, though. For one, some organizations might find that too much change accumulates between the 6-month releases and that there's less risk in releasing more frequent and smaller changes from the trunk. Although this makes sense with a lot of software projects, OpenStack is developed by a number of loosely coordinated teams, and managing the dependencies between the development streams of each project is a complicated task. Automated testing on the trunk attempts to ensure that a change in Nova doesn't break a feature in Neutron, but the bulk of manual integration testing happens for the coordinated stable releases.

Although it's possible that an organization may want to take all the changes from the trunk before they make it down to the stable branches, it's more likely that they'll be interested in only one or two important features that haven't made it to the branches. For example, many of the teams that we have worked with were interested in leveraging external IPAM systems similar to the one provided by Infoblox long before the feature was implemented in Neutron (in the Liberty release). We've seen other situations in which an organization wanted to pull in a Cinder driver for a new SAN device before it was accepted upstream. For these use cases, it makes more sense to start off with a packaged distribution of one of the stable branches and then create a custom package only for the component that has the desired feature backported to it from the trunk.

Community distributions

After each stable release of OpenStack, the software from the resulting stable branches is packaged up by maintainers from three of the major community Linux distributions into the native format for their distribution. These distributions of OpenStack allow users of those distributions to install the software (and its dependencies) using the usual mechanism for that distribution. These distributors also provide documentation at `http://openstack.org` on how to install and configure the software on their particular distribution.

Most organizations will choose a community distribution based on the Linux distribution that they're most comfortable with. For example, organizations that typically use the Ubuntu Linux distribution will use the Ubuntu OpenStack distribution as well. It's worth noting that the community distributions of OpenStack will work with the commercially supported variants of both openSUSE and CentOS; it's not uncommon for an organization to pay for support for Red Hat Enterprise Linux but to use the community-supported CentOS distribution of OpenStack (RDO).

The choice of community distribution may also have an effect on the availability of installation mechanisms. For example, the Packstack installation tool that we used in Chapter 1, *Introducing OpenStack*, is specific to the CentOS distribution of OpenStack (RDO). The Ubuntu and openSUSE distributions have other tools to install the OpenStack software. However, the Puppet, Chef, and Ansible mechanisms for deploying OpenStack are distribution (and operating system) agnostic. For example, it is possible to deploy OpenStack on the Ubuntu and CentOS distributions using the same Puppet modules.

Commercially supported distributions

Although there are only three major community-supported distributions of OpenStack available, there are a myriad of commercially-supported distributions available. A list of these distributions and their certification status is available at: http://openstack.org. Distributions that have passed specific load and performance-based tempest tests are certified in the same way as managed service providers. Commercially supported distributions are frequently based on the community-supported distributions. However, there are a few reasons that organizations prefer them to the community distributions.

The first major driver is *support*. Most companies that provide support for OpenStack require the customer to use their commercially supported distribution so that they can ensure that the customer is using software that has passed through a certification and testing process. For example, Red Hat takes the packages from each RDO release and runs them through a detailed test plan before releasing them as a Red Hat Enterprise Linux OpenStack platform. When a customer identifies an issue with a particular OpenStack component, Red Hat can add that issue to the test plan to prevent regressions in future releases. In addition, customers may choose different commercial distributions for ease of use, quality of support, or any additional software that may be included with the distribution.

Organizations may also choose a commercially supported distribution over a community-supported distribution because the distribution has added functionality that hasn't been released by the distributor as open source. These enhancements tend to be aimed towards speeding up the deployment of OpenStack clouds or improving the manageability of deployments with additional reporting and dashboards.

Compute hardware considerations

Selecting a hardware platform for compute infrastructure in OpenStack is similar to selecting a hardware platform for any other workload in the data center. Some organizations have a brand loyalty to a particular vendor based on reputation, past performance, or business arrangements, and some organizations ask hardware vendors to bid on projects as they come up. A small number of organizations choose to assemble their own systems from components, but most OpenStack deployments use the same commodity systems that would be deployed to run any other Linux workload.

With that said, we've definitely seen hardware configurations that work well with OpenStack and ones that had to be reconfigured after the fact. We'll try to help you avoid that second purchase order in this section.

Hypervisor selection

The majority of installations use either the Xen or KVM hypervisors, but there are a number of other hypervisors available for use with Nova. Both the Hyper-V and VMware hypervisors are supported as compute platforms. Bare-metal systems can be provisioned through Nova (Ironic project) and various drivers for containers have come and gone over the life of OpenStack. Running containers in OpenStack is a topic of great interest lately, and the OpenStack Magnum project has emerged as the current favorite model for their deployment within OpenStack.

Whether to pick the Xen or KVM hypervisor is almost a religious matter for some people. The KVM hypervisor is the most broadly used hypervisor on Linux, and it has support for a wide range of advanced features, such as PCI-passthrough, NUMA zone pinning, and live migration. Proponents of Xen will point out that performance on older hardware has traditionally been better with Xen. They will also point out that large cloud providers such as Amazon and Rackspace have picked the Xen hypervisor over the KVM hypervisor for their deployments. However, adoption continues to wane for the Xen hypervisor. Based on the 2017 OpenStack User Survey report, 86% of OpenStack clouds in production are using KVM and only 11% are using Xen. KVM is the default and most widely used hypervisor, and unless your organization has a strong motivation to pick the Xen hypervisor, we strongly recommend that you use it over any other hypervisor.

A number of good arguments can be made for using VMware ESX as the hypervisor in OpenStack instead of KVM. Almost every large IT shop has a great deal of experience with ESX and vSphere, and using ESX as the hypervisor for an OpenStack deployment can ease the barrier for entry to OpenStack for teams that don't want to certify or train up on a new virtualization technology. ESX-based deployments are prescriptive; there is only one Cinder driver and one Neutron driver supported with ESX. From this perspective, choosing ESX allows an organization to focus on the integration and operational aspects of OpenStack without worrying too much about the architecture.

The same reasons that make ESX a good choice for some organizations make it a poor choice for many organizations, though. The prescriptive approach limits available options in the storage and network space. One of the strongest aspects of OpenStack is the heterogeneity of the ecosystem and the ability to dynamically add new types of infrastructure under a common API. For this reason, we'll be focusing our work in this book on the use of the KVM hypervisor. Most of the considerations we address in this section will also apply to the Xen hypervisor.

Sizing the hardware to match the workload

As we mentioned at the start of this chapter, while an iterative approach for developing and deploying software is a best practice, an iterative approach for purchasing hardware has the potential to kill your private cloud initiative. It's crucial to get the hardware right at the first time so that you can line up the appropriate discounts from your hardware vendor and set the appropriate budget at the start of the project. Sizing is often difficult for these projects though, as it can be difficult to anticipate the requirements of the workload ahead of time. This is one of the reasons that it's so important to get the application owners involved early in the project—they'll be able to anticipate what their application requirements will be, and that will inform the sizing process.

The first step in the sizing process is to define standard instance sizes. These are referred to as flavors in the Nova parlance. Out of the box, Nova ships with a set of "m1" flavors, which correspond roughly to Amazon EC2 instance types. A flavor has three prominent parameters—the number of virtual CPUs, the amount of memory, and the amount of ephemeral disk storage. Organizations typically define two or three flavors, based on the anticipated workload. Three common flavors are the 1×2, 2×4, and 4×8 sizes, which refer to the number of vCPUs and gigabytes of memory. The ephemeral disk size is typically the same, regardless of CPU and memory configuration—it should equate to the expected size of a root disk of the organization's standard Glance images. For example, a 2×4 with the Red Hat Enterprise Linux 7 qcow2 image would have two virtual CPUs, 4 gigabytes of memory, and a 20 gigabyte ephemeral disk.

Once the flavors have been defined, the next step is to determine the acceptable overcommit ratio for a given environment. Each of the major hardware vendors publishes virtual performance benchmark results that can be used as a starting point for this ratio. These benchmarks are available at http://spec.org/ in the virtualization category. Working through these benchmarks, two simple rules emerge: never overcommit memory and always overcommit CPU up to 10 times. Following these rules allows you to determine the optimal amount of memory in a given piece of compute hardware. For example, a compute node with 36 physical cores can support up to 360 virtual cores of compute. If we use the preceding flavors, we'll see a ratio of 2 gigabytes of RAM to each virtual core. The optimum amount of memory in this compute node would top out somewhere around 720 GB (2 GB x 10 x 36 cores).

There's typically a dramatic price difference in tiers of memory, and it often makes sense to configure the system with less than the optimum amount of memory. Let's assume that it is only economical to configure our 36 core compute node with 512 GB of memory. The next two items to consider are network bandwidth and available ephemeral storage. This is where it helps to understand the target workload. 512 GB of memory would support 256 1x2 instances, 128 2x4 instances, or 64 4x8 instances. That gives us a maximum ephemeral disk requirement between 1.2 and 5 TB, assuming a 20 GB Glance image. That's a pretty large discrepancy. If we feel confident that the bulk of our instances will be 2x4, we can size for around 128 instances, which gives us a requirement of 2.5 TB of disk space for ephemeral storage. There's some leeway in there as well - ephemeral storage is thin-provisioned with the KVM hypervisor and it's unlikely that we'll consume the full capacity. However, if we use persistent storage options such as Ceph, SAN, iSCSI, or NFS for image, instance, or object storage, planning for capacity becomes more complicated. Even though you're determining your flavor CPU, memory, and ephemeral disk sizing, you will need to include persistent disk space for root volumes. If these volumes are stored on the same appliances/clusters as your glance and object storage, great care must be taken to ensure consistent elasticity.

The last major item to consider when selecting compute hardware is the available bandwidth on the compute node. Most of the systems we work with today have two 10 gigabit bonded interfaces dedicated to instance traffic. Dividing the available bandwidth by the number of anticipated instances allows us to determine whether an additional set of interfaces is required. Dividing 10 gigabits by 128 instances gives us roughly 75 megabits of available average bandwidth for each instance. This is more than sufficient for most web and database workloads.

Considerations for performance-intensive workloads

The guidelines given earlier work well for development, web, or database workloads. Some workloads, particularly **Network Function Virtualization** (**NFV**) workloads, have very specific performance requirements that need to be addressed in the hardware selection process. A few improvements to the scheduling of instances have been added to the Nova compute service in order to enable these workloads.

The first improvement allows for passing through a PCI device directly from the hardware into the instance. In standard OpenStack Neutron networking, packets traverse a set of bridges between the instance's virtual interface and the actual network interface. The amount of overhead in this virtual networking is significant, as each packet consumes CPU resources each time it traverses an interface or switch. This performance overhead can be eliminated by allowing the virtual machine to have direct access to the network device via a technology named **SR-IOV**. SR-IOV allows a single network adapter to appear as multiple network adapters to the operating system. Each of these virtual network adapters (referred to as virtual functions or VFs) can be directly associated with a virtual instance.

The second improvement allows the Nova scheduler to specify the CPU and memory zone for an instance on a compute node that has **Non-Uniform Memory Access** (**NUMA**). In these NUMA systems, a certain amount of memory is located closer to a certain set of processor cores. A performance penalty occurs when processes access memory pages in a region that is nonadjacent. Another significant performance penalty occurs when processes move from one memory zone to another. To get around these performance penalties, the Nova scheduler has the ability to pin the virtual CPUs of an instance to physical cores in the underlying compute node. It also has the ability to restrict a virtual instance to a given memory region associated with those virtual CPUs, effectively constraining the instance to a specified NUMA zone.

The last major performance improvement in the Nova Compute service is around memory page allocation. By default, the Linux operating system allocates memory in 4 kilobyte pages on 64-bit Intel systems. While this makes a lot of sense for traditional workloads (it maps to the size of a typical filesystem block), it can have an adverse effect on memory allocation performance in virtual machines. The Linux operating system also allows 2 megabyte- and 1 gigabyte-sized memory pages, commonly referred to as huge pages. The Kilo release of OpenStack included support for using huge pages to back virtual instances.

The combination of PCI-passthrough, CPU and memory pinning, and huge page support allows for dramatic performance improvements for virtual instances in OpenStack, and they are required for workloads such as NFV. They have some implications for hardware selection that are worth noting, though. Typical NFV instances will expect to have an entire NUMA zone dedicated to them. As such, these are typically very large flavors and the flavors tend to be application-specific. They're also hardware-specific—if your flavor specifies that the instance needs 16 virtual CPUs and 32 gigabytes of memory, then the hardware needs to have a NUMA zone with 16 physical cores and 32 gigabytes of memory available. Also, if that NUMA zone has an addition 32 gigabytes of memory configured, it will be unavailable to the rest of the system as the instance has exclusive access to that zone.

Network design

The network requirements for a particular OpenStack deployment also vary widely depending on the workload. OpenStack also typically provides an organization's first experience with **Software-Defined Networking (SDN)**, which complicates the design process for the physical and virtual networks. Cloud Architects should lean heavily on their peers in the network architecture team in the planning of the network.

Providing network segmentation

OpenStack's roots in the public cloud provider space have left a significant impact on the network design at both the physical and virtual layer. In a public cloud deployment, the relationship between the tenant workload and the provider workload is based on a total absence of trust. In these deployments, the users and applications in the tenant space have no network access to any of the systems that are providing the underlying compute, network, and storage. Some access has to be provided for the end users to reach the API endpoints of the OpenStack cloud though, and so the control plane is typically multihomed on a set of physically segmented networks. This adds a layer of complexity to the deployment, but it has proven to be a best practice from a security standpoint in private cloud deployments as well.

There are typically four types of networks in an OpenStack deployment. The first is a network that is used to access the OpenStack APIs from the internet in the case of a public cloud or the intranet in the case of a private cloud. In most deployments, only the load balancers have an address on this network. This allows tight control and auditing of traffic coming in from the internet. This network is often referred to as the **external network**. The second type of network is a private network that is used for communication between the OpenStack control plane and the compute infrastructure. The message bus and database are exposed on this network, and traffic is typically not routed in or out of this network. This network is referred to as the **management network**.

Two more additional private networks are typically created to carry network and storage traffic between the compute, network, and storage nodes. These networks are broken out for quality of service as much as security and are optional, depending on whether the deployment is using SDN or network-attached storage. The segment dedicated to tenant networking is frequently referred to as the **tenant network** or the underlay network. Depending on the size of the deployment, there may be one or more of these underlay networks. The storage network is, not surprisingly, referred to as the **storage network**.

One last class of network is required for tenant workloads to access the internet or intranet in most deployments. Commonly referred to as the **provider network**, this is a physical network that is modeled in Neutron to provide network ports on a physical network. Floating IPs, which can be dynamically assigned to instances, are drawn from the provider networks. In some deployments, instances will be allowed to use ports from provider networks directly, without passing through the tenant network and router. Organizations that would like to have the Neutron API available, but don't want to implement SDN frequently, use this pattern of modeling the physical infrastructure in Neutron with provider networks. This allows them to use traditional physical switches and routers but still provide dynamic virtual interfaces.

Software-defined networking

SDN is one of the key capabilities that differentiates OpenStack from traditional virtualization deployments. SDN uses tunneling technology to create a virtual network topology on top of a physical network topology. The virtual (overlay) networks can be shared or tenant-specific. Tenants can define their own layer 2 segments and routers, they can specify network-specific DNS and DHCP services, and some deployments allow for layer 4 services such as load balancing and firewalling to be defined as well. Neutron was created with a plugin-based architecture, and plugins exist for software and hardware-based SDN products. A reference implementation built around Open vSwitch is also provided for testing and lab work.

SDN vendors tend to differentiate themselves in three areas. The first is around the resiliency of their solution. Organizations evaluating SDN technologies should pay attention to how the layer 3 routers are made highly available in a given topology and how packet flows are impacted by component failure. The second is around the management interface of a given solution. Most of the SDN vendors will have an eye-catching and useful user interface to use to debug packet flows within the tenant networks. The third factor to consider is performance. In our experience, this is the deciding factor for most organizations. There are typically large differences in the performance of these solutions, and attention should be focused on this during **Proof of Concepts (PoCs)**.

Physical network design

No discussion of OpenStack networking would be complete without the mention of the spine-leaf physical network architecture. Spine-leaf is an alternative to the traditional multitier network architecture, which is made up of a set of core, aggregation, and access layers. Spine-leaf introduces a modification to the design of the aggregation layer in order to reduce the number of hops between servers that are attached to different access switches. The aggregation layer becomes a spine in which every access switch (the leaf) can reach every other access switch through a single spine switch. This architecture is often considered a prerequisite for horizontally scalable cloud workloads, which are focused more on traffic between instances (east-west traffic) than traffic between instances and the internet (north-south traffic).

The primary impact that spine-leaf network design has on OpenStack deployments is that layer 2 networks are typically terminated at the spine—meaning that subnets cannot stretch from leaf to leaf. This has a couple of implications. First, virtual IPs cannot migrate from leaf to leaf and thus the external network is constrained to a single leaf. If the leaf boundary is the top-of-rack switch, this places all the load balancers for a given control plane within a single failure zone (the rack). Secondly, provider networks need to be physically attached to each compute node within an OpenStack region if instances are going to be directly attached to them. This limitation can constrain an OpenStack region to the size of a leaf. Once again, if the leaf boundary is the top-of-rack switch, this makes for very small regions, which lead to an unusually high ratio of control to compute nodes.

We've seen a couple of different approaches on how to implement spine-leaf within OpenStack installations given these limitations. The first is to simply stretch L2 networks across the leaves in a given deployment. The only networks which require stretching are the external API network and the provider networks. If instances are not going to be directly attached to the provider networks (that is, if floating IPs are used for external connectivity), then these networks only need to be stretched across a failure zone to ensure that the loss of a single rack doesn't bring down the control plane. Deployments that chose to stretch L2 across racks typically group racks into pods of three or more racks, which then become the leaf boundary. The second approach that we've seen used is to create tunnels within the spine, which simulate stretched L2 subnets across the top of rack switches. Either way, collaboration between the network architecture team and the cloud architecture team should lead to a solution that is supportable by the organization.

The concept of availability zones was introduced to Neutron in the Mitaka release of OpenStack (`https://blueprints.launchpad.net/neutron/+spec/add-availability-zone`). Availability zones allow the OpenStack administrator to expose leaf boundaries to the Nova scheduler, which allows Nova to decide where to place workloads based on the network topology. Although not in wide use yet, this feature will provide much more flexibility for OpenStack architects when deploying with a spine-leaf network architecture.

Storage design

As compute hardware has become less expensive over the past few years, fewer and fewer workloads are constrained by a lack of processor or memory performance. Instead, most workloads are tuned so that they are constrained on I/O—particularly, storage I/O. OpenStack workloads typically separate the operating system storage from the application storage and Cinder, and the different object storage projects provide mechanisms to present many different kinds of storage with a single interface. This capability allows tenants to choose the storage that matches their application's requirements. In addition to Cinder providing persistence for applications, block storage and object storage also provide storage persistence for instances and allow instance live migration, backup, and recovery.

Ephemeral storage

Ephemeral storage is the storage that is consumed when a Glance image is copied locally to a compute node to instantiate a virtual instance. Glance images are typically sparse and tend to be less than 1 gigabyte in size. When instantiated, images provide the root disk for an instance's operating system. These are also sparsely provisioned, but typically grow up to 10, 20, or 40 gigabytes in size. In traditional OpenStack deployments, ephemeral storage is provided by the compute node's internal disks, and when a compute node fails or an instance is terminated, the storage is lost or reclaimed. These days, many organizations will choose to place ephemeral storage on shared storage.

There are two main reasons to use shared storage for ephemeral instance storage. The first reason is to make those ephemeral instances a little less ephemeral by providing for a live migration capability for instances. With local-only ephemeral storage, any reboot of a compute node will terminate the instances it is currently hosting. If the instance is backed by shared storage (typically NFS or software-based storage such as Ceph), it can be migrated to another compute node that has access to the same storage without downtime. This allows cloud operators to put compute nodes in a *maintenance mode* so that they can be patched. When the compute nodes are ready to host workloads again, the instances can be rebalanced across the nodes. Having a live copy of the instance is also useful in the case of a compute node failure. Instances backed by shared storage can be evacuated to healthy compute nodes without losing state.

The second reason that shared storage is attractive for ephemeral storage is that some storage backends allow deduplication between Glance images and running instances. In a traditional instance life cycle, there isn't a huge need for deduplication between the images and the instances. However, if there is a deduplication capability, it allows operators to use instance snapshots as backups. Instances can be backed up on a regular basis without consuming an inordinate amount of shared storage. OpenStack allows quiescing guest operating systems during snapshot operations to enable this kind of *live backup* capability.

Block storage

Using shared storage for ephemeral storage is one way to achieve a persistence capability for virtual instances, but the more traditional way is to instantiate a Glance image on a Cinder volume. Instances that are backed by Cinder volumes can be live-migrated, live-snapshotted, and evacuated with their state intact. There are Cinder drivers for almost every major storage product on the market these days, and it is common to configure multiple backends within a single OpenStack deployment. This allows the OpenStack tenant to choose an appropriate backend for their workload. For example, a database instance might have its operating system reside on a relatively inexpensive ephemeral disk, but locates the data on a highly performant SAN storage attached by a fiber channel. If the instance fails, the root disk is discarded and a new instance attaches itself to the persistent Cinder volume. Cinder volumes are also attractive as root disks for instances that are being migrated from traditional virtualization platforms. The user experience for Cinder-backed instances is very similar to these platforms.

The selection of storage backends for Cinder implementations is a relatively straightforward process. Cloud architects will want to leverage the relationships and knowledge that an organization's storage architects already have. Storage devices are relatively expensive, and PoCs should be run on existing hardware devices where possible. Cinder drivers for commonplace devices, such as NetApp filers and EMC SANs, have some interesting features, which can be proven out in a lab. Vendors of more exotic hardware devices are typically willing to lend hardware for PoCs as well.

Most of the organizations that we've worked with have tested software-based storage as a part of their OpenStack implementations, and many have gone on to adopt software-based storage for at least one of their storage tiers. Ceph, in particular, has a tight integration with OpenStack for image, ephemeral, and block storage. Ceph has the advantage of providing deduplication when used in this configuration. This, combined with its usage of commodity hardware, makes it an extremely attractive option from a cost perspective.

Object storage

Swift was one of the first two services in OpenStack, and object storage was the original mechanism for persistence within OpenStack (and Amazon) clouds. As OpenStack has been adopted for more and more traditional workloads, object storage has lost a lot of its relevance. In fact, many of the OpenStack deployments that we work on in the Enterprise space don't include object storage in the initial release.

An easy way to take an *if you build it they will come* approach to object storage is to leverage it for storing Glance images. Although a few of your tenants may come to your OpenStack deployment with applications that can persist their data over an S3-compatible interface, almost all of them can use the snapshot capability in Nova to improve their experience on the platform. Storing Glance images in Swift makes them highly available and provides an opportunity to colocate them with the compute infrastructure, dramatically improving network performance.

Object storage backend selection is highly dependent on block and ephemeral storage selection. If you are using Ceph for block storage, using Ceph for object storage greatly simplifies administration of the platform. NetApp provides an integration with Swift, and it may be advantageous to choose it instead if using NetApp for block storage. Swift is also the default object storage provider in OpenStack, and it makes sense to use it in heterogeneous environments from that perspective. In our experience, object storage backends are not subjected to the same kind of scrutiny as block storage backends in the storage selection process. This may be because many object storage systems are less about performance and more about low-cost options to store frequently read data versus a lot of heavy I/O.

Expanding the initial deployment

To properly evaluate the different compute, network, and storage options we've discussed in this chapter, an expanded OpenStack deployment with dedicated roles for different physical systems is required. Separating the compute functions from the control functions allows us to properly test different types of compute hardware. Separating storage functions from compute and control functions allows us to properly test different disk, NAS, or SAN configurations. In this section, we'll split out the roles we deployed in Chapter 1, *Introducing OpenStack*, to three physical systems. Each of these systems will be assigned a role, which we'll call a host group.

Updating the design document

Our first task is to update the design document from Chapter 1, *Introducing OpenStack*, with a set of definitions of our host groups. These definitions should be included at the start of the *Physical architecture* section of the document. We'll use the following host groups in this expanded PoC.

Cloud controller

The cloud controller system provides the API services, scheduling services, and Horizon dashboard services for the OpenStack deployment.

Compute node

The compute node systems act as KVM hypervisors and run the `nova-compute` and `openvswitch-agent` services.

The *Physical architecture* section of the design document should also contain a section on the physical network architecture of the deployment. In this section, each of the segmented networks should be defined. Connectivity for each physical host to each network should also be defined.

The Packstack installation tool doesn't allow the specification of an external network for API traffic. As such, we'll use three physical networks in this deployment: a management network that is routable to the intranet, a provider network that provides floating IPs for the instances, and a tenant network for instance traffic. The following network definitions should be added to the *Physical architecture* section.

Management network

The management network is used for the private communication between all nodes in the OpenStack deployment. This network is also used to carry tenant and storage traffic in this deployment.

Provider network

The provider network is used to provide public ports for tenant instances in this deployment. The cloud controller node has a port on this network segment.

Tenant network

The tenant network carries the tenant network traffic in the deployment. It acts as an underlay network for the SDN tunnels. Compute nodes and controller nodes have ports on this network segment.

A network diagram should also be added to the *Physical architecture* section. The following diagram describes the deployment in this chapter:

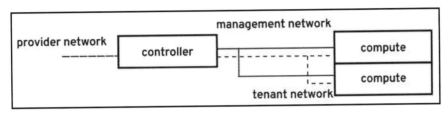

Updating the deployment plan

The deployment plan for our lab environment needs to be updated to reflect the additional hardware and network configuration. The hardware table should be updated first to include the assignment of a role to each piece of hardware. For example, consider the following table:

Hostname	Model	CPU	Memory	Disk	Network	Host Group
controller1	DL380	16	256 GB	500 GB	2x10 GB	Cloud controller
compute1	DL380	32	512 GB	2 TB	2x10 GB	Compute node
compute2	DL380	32	512 GB	2 TB	2x10 GB	Compute node

Next, update the network table to reflect the new nodes and networks:

Hostname	Interface	MAC	IP	Network
controller1	eth0	3C:97:0E:BF:6C:78	192.168.0.10	Management
	eth0.100	3C:97:0E:BF:6C:78	10.0.0.10	Provider
	eth0.200	3C:97:0E:BF:6C:78	172.16.0.10	Tenant
compute1	eth0	3C:97:0E:BF:6C:80	192.168.0.100	Management
	eth0.200	3C:97:0E:BF:6C:80	172.16.0.100	Tenant
compute2	eth0	3C:97:0E:BF:6C:81	192.168.0.101	Management
	eth0.200	3C:97:0E:BF:6C:81	172.16.0.101	Tenant

It can also be helpful to include the following table, which describes each network for the deployment:

Network	VLAN ID	Subnet	Gateway
Management		192.168.0.0/24	192.168.0.1
Provider	100	10.0.0.0/24	10.0.0.1
Tenant	200	172.16.0.0/24	172.16.0.1

Installing OpenStack with the new configuration

In Chapter 1, *Introducing OpenStack*, we ran packstack with the all-in-one option, taking the defaults for a test installation. Packstack has the ability to save the default options into a configuration file that can then be edited with a text editor. We'll use this ability in this chapter to create a reusable configuration. Also, Packstack has the ability to apply the generated puppet manifests to remote machines over SSH. For this to work, you will need to be able to access SSH from the controller machine (where we'll be running Packstack) to the other machines in the deployment. It's a good idea to test this out prior to running Packstack.

To begin, start by installing a fresh copy of the operating system on the three servers that we outlined in the hardware table in the deployment plan. Each system needs to have the network interfaces specified in the network table configured before deployment, and all the requirements specified in the deployment plan will also need to be met (that is, the network manager needs to be disabled and the RDO repository needs to be enabled).

Execute the following command on the cloud controller (controller1) to generate an answer file. We'll use this as a template for our deployment configuration:

```
# packstack -gen-answer-file=packstack-answers.txt
```

Next, edit the packstack-answers.txt file, updating the following parameters:

Parameter	Example	Description
CONFIG_CONTROLLER_HOST	192.168.0.10	IP address of the cloud controller on the management network

CONFIG_COMPUTE_HOSTS	192.168.0.100, 192.168.0.101	IP addresses of the compute nodes on the management network
CONFIG_NETWORK_HOSTS	192.168.0.10	IP address of the cloud controller on the management network
CONFIG_AMQP_HOST	192.168.0.10	IP address of the cloud controller on the management network
CONFIG_MARIADB_HOST	192.168.0.10	IP address of the cloud controller on the management network
CONFIG_NEUTRON_OVS_BRIDGE_MAPPINGS	vlan100:br-vlan100	A mapping of neutron networks to OVS bridges for the provider network
CONFIG_NEUTRON_OVS_BRIDGE_IFACES	br-vlan100:eth0.100	A mapping of OVS bridges to physical interfaces for the provider network
CONFIG_NEUTRON_OVS_TUNNEL_IF	eth0.200	An interface to use for the tenant network
CONFIG_PROVISION_DEMO_FLOATRANGE	10.0.0.128/25	A floating IP range to use on the provider network

Now, run `packstack` with the new configuration:

```
# packstack --answer-file=packstack-answers.txt
```

When the installation completes, the OpenStack deployment should be verified using the same steps as in the previous chapter. Service distribution can be verified by querying the Nova and Neutron schedulers:

```
# nova service-list
```

This command will output a table of all running compute services, the host they're running on, and their status. The output should show the `nova-cert`, `nova-consoleauth`, `nova-scheduler`, and `nova-conductor` services running on compute1 and the `nova-compute` service running on compute1 and compute2:

```
# neutron agent-list
```

This command will output a similar table of all running network services. The output should show the Metadata, L3, and DHCP agents running on controller1 and the Open vSwitch agent running on controller1, compute1, and compute2.

Summary

OpenStack deployments are often compared with snowflakes. There are so many different ways to combine the various supported compute, storage, and network configurations that no deployment resembles any other deployment. This analogy is frequently used in frustration at companies that offer commercial support for OpenStack—the diversity of deployments makes supporting customers extremely difficult. Many of the clients we work with have also expressed frustration at the myriad of options available. On the other hand, most of the people who have been running OpenStack for a while realize the value of having so many options. It allows them to continually provide new services and capabilities to their customers under a common interface.

In this chapter, we walked through each of the three major areas of technology in OpenStack—compute, network, and storage. In each area, we've broadly described the choices available and provided some guidance on how to approach the decision process. We've also expanded our deployment documentation and the deployment itself to incorporate some of the information covered in this chapter. This basic deployment can be expanded upon and should provide enough diversity to be used to test out different compute, network, and storage technologies in the lab before making a purchasing decision.

In the next chapter, you'll look at how to take this simple deployment and make it more robust with the addition of high-availability software.

Further reading

Please refer to the following links for further reading:

- **The list of Neutron Plugins**: `https://wiki.openstack.org/wiki/Neutron#Plugins`
- **The list of Cinder Drivers**: `https://wiki.openstack.org/wiki/CinderSupportMatrix`
- **The list of OpenStack Distributions**: `https://www.openstack.org/marketplace/distros/`
- **Standard Performance Evaluation Comparison for Virtualization**: `http://spec.org/virt_sc2013/`

3
Planning for Failure and Success

In this chapter, we'll be walking through how to architect your cloud to avoid hardware and software failures. The OpenStack control plane is composed of web services, application services, database services, and a message bus. All of these tiers require different approaches to make them highly available and some organizations will already have defined architectures for each of the services. We've seen that customers either reuse those existing patterns or adopt new ones that are specific to the OpenStack platform. Both of these approaches make sense, depending on the scale of the deployment. Many successful deployments actually implement a blend of these.

For example, if your organization already has a supported pattern for highly available MySQL databases, you might choose that pattern instead of the one outlined in this chapter. If your organization doesn't have a pattern for highly available MongoDB, you might have to architect a new one.

This chapter is divided into the following topics:

- Highly available control plane strategies and patterns
- OpenStack regions, cells, and availability zones
- Updating the design document and implementing the design

Building a highly available control plane

Back in the Folsom and Grizzly days, coming up with a **high availability** (HA) design for the OpenStack control plane was something of a dark art. Many of the technologies recommended in the first iterations of the OpenStack high availability guide were specific to the Ubuntu distribution of Linux and were unavailable on the Red Hat Enterprise Linux-derived distributions.

The now-standard cluster resource manager (Pacemaker) was unsupported by Red Hat at that time. As such, architects using Ubuntu might use one set of software, those using CentOS or RHEL might use another set of software, and those using a Rackspace or Mirantis distribution might use yet another set of software. However, these days, the technology stack has converged and the HA pattern is largely consistent, regardless of the distribution used.

That being said, many OpenStack deployments are now starting to use container technologies such as Docker, LXC, and Kubernetes for running at least the control plane web services. These technologies open up many new possibilities for ensuring the availability of these services. We'll talk more about containers in a later chapter.

About failure and success

When we design a highly available OpenStack control plane, we're looking to mitigate two different scenarios. The first is failure. When a physical piece of hardware dies, we want to make sure that we recover without human interaction and continue to provide service to our users. The second and perhaps more important scenario is success.

Software systems always work as designed and tested until humans start using them. While our automated test suites will try to launch a reasonable number of virtual objects, humans are guaranteed to attempt to launch an unreasonable number. Also, many of the OpenStack projects we've worked on have grown far past their expected size and need to be expanded on the fly.

There are a few different types of success scenarios that we need to plan for when architecting an OpenStack cloud.

First, we need to plan for a growth in the number of instances. This is relatively straightforward. Each additional instance grows the size of the database, it grows the amount of metering data in Ceilometer, and, most importantly, it will grow the number of compute nodes. Adding compute nodes and reporting puts strain on the message bus, which is typically the limiting factor in the size of OpenStack regions or cells. We'll talk more about this when we talk about dividing up OpenStack clouds into regions, cells, and availability zones.

The second type of growth we need to plan for is an increase in the number of API calls. Deployments that support **Continuous Integration (CI)** development environments might have (relatively) small compute requirements, but CI typically brings up and tears down environments rapidly. This will generate a large amount of API traffic, which in turn generates a large amount of database and message traffic.

In hosting environments, end users might also manually generate a lot of API traffic as they bring up and down instances, or manually check the status of deployments they've already launched. While a service catalog might check the status of instances it has launched on a regular basis, humans tend to hit refresh on their browsers in an erratic fashion. Automated testing of the platform has a tendency to grossly underestimate this kind of behavior.

With that in mind, any pattern that we adopt will need to provide for the following requirements:

- API services must continue to be available during a hardware failure in the control plane
- The systems that provide API services must be horizontally scalable (and ideally elastic) to respond to unanticipated demands
- The database services must be vertically or horizontally scalable to respond to unanticipated growth of the platform
- The message bus can either be vertically or horizontally scaled depending on the technology chosen

Finally, every system has its limits. These limits should be defined in the architecture documentation so that capacity planning can account for them. At some point, the control plane has scaled as far as it can and a second control plane should be deployed to provide additional capacity. Although OpenStack is designed to be massively scalable, it isn't designed to be infinitely scalable.

High availability patterns for the control plane

There are three approaches commonly used in OpenStack deployments these days for achieving the high availability of the control plane.

The first is the simplest. Take the single-node cloud controller that we deployed in Chapter 2, *Architecting the Cloud*, virtualize it, and then make the virtual machine highly available using either VMware clustering or Linux clustering. While this option is simple and it provides for failure scenarios, it scales vertically (not horizontally) and doesn't provide for success scenarios. As such, it should only be used in regions with a limited number of compute nodes and a limited number of API calls. In practice, this method isn't used frequently and we won't spend any more time on it here.

The second pattern provides for HA, but is not horizontal scalability. This is the **active/passive** scenario described in the OpenStack high availability guide. At Red Hat, we used this a lot with our Folsom and Grizzly deployments, but moved away from it starting with Havana.

It's similar to the virtualization solution described earlier but instead of relying on VMware clustering or Linux clustering to restart a failed virtual machine, it relies on Linux clustering to restart failed services on a second cloud controller node, also running the same subset of services. This pattern doesn't provide for success scenarios in the web tier, but can still be used in the database and messaging tiers. Some networking services may still need to be provided as active/passive as well.

The third HA pattern available to OpenStack architectures is the **active/active** pattern. In this pattern, services are horizontally scaled out behind a load balancing service or appliance, which is active/passive. As a general rule, most OpenStack services should be enabled as active/active where possible to allow for success scenarios while mitigating failure scenarios. Ideally, active/active services can be scaled out elastically without service disruption by simply adding additional control plane nodes.

Both the active/passive and active/active designs require clustering software to determine the health of services and the hosts on which they run. In this chapter, we'll be using Pacemaker as the cluster manager. Some architects may choose to use Keepalived instead of Pacemaker.

In addition to these three scenarios, there are always limitations on scaling OpenStack services beyond a certain limit. As previously mentioned, the messaging bus is typically the first service to see issues with regard to scale; however, it's not the only place. It is always a best practice to monitor the responsiveness of all of the OpenStack services, as well as performing scale testing using tools such as Tempest and/or Rally in a simulated environment, to assess the impact of demand growth on your OpenStack clouds.

Active/passive service configuration

In the active/passive service configuration, the service is configured and deployed to two or more physical systems. The service is associated with a **Virtual IP (VIP)** address. A cluster resource manager (normally Pacemaker) is used to ensure that the service and its VIP are enabled on only one of the two systems at any point in time. The resource manager may be configured to favor one of the machines over the other.

When the machine that the service is running on fails, the resource manager first ensures that the failed machine is no longer running and then it starts the service on the second machine. Ensuring that the failed machine is no longer running is accomplished through a process known as **fencing**. Fencing usually entails powering off the machine using the management interface on the BIOS. The fence agent may also talk to a power supply connected to the failed server to ensure that the system is down.

Some services (such as the Glance image registry) require shared storage to operate. If the storage is network-based, such as NFS, the storage may be mounted on both the active and the passive nodes simultaneously. If the storage is block-based, such as iSCSI, the storage will only be mounted on the active node and the resource manager will ensure that the storage migrates with the service and the VIP.

Active/active service configuration

Most of the OpenStack API services are designed to be run on more than one system simultaneously. This configuration, the active/active configuration, requires a load balancer to spread traffic across each of the active services. The load balancer manages the VIP for the service and ensures that the backend systems are listening before forwarding traffic to them. The cluster manager ensures that the VIP is only active on one node at a time. The backend services may or may not be managed by the cluster manager in the active/active configuration. Service or system failure is detected by the load balancer and failed services are brought out of rotation.

There are a few different advantages to the active/active service configuration, which are as follows:

- The first advantage is that it allows for horizontal scalability. If additional capacity is needed for a given service, a new system can be brought up that is running the service and it can be added into rotation behind the load balancer without any downtime. The control plane may also be scaled down without downtime in the event that it was over-provisioned.
- The second advantage is that active/active services have a much shorter mean time to recovery. Fencing operations often take up to two minutes and fencing is required before the cluster resource manager will move a service from a failed system to a healthy one. Load balancers can immediately detect system failure and stop sending requests to unresponsive nodes while the cluster manager fences them in the background.

Whenever possible, architects should employ the active/active pattern for the control plane services.

OpenStack service specifics

In this section, we'll walk through each of the OpenStack services and outline the HA strategy for them. While most of the services can be configured as active/active behind a load balancer, some of them must be configured as active/passive and others may be configured as active/passive. Some of the configuration is dependent on a particular version of OpenStack as well, especially Ceilometer, Heat, and Neutron. The following details are current as of the Pike release of OpenStack.

OpenStack web services

As a general rule, all of the web services and the Horizon dashboard may be run active/active. These include the API services for Keystone, Glance, Nova, Cinder, Neutron, Heat, and Ceilometer. The scheduling services for Nova, Cinder, Neutron, Heat, and Ceilometer may also be deployed active/active. These services do not require a load balancer, as they respond to requests on the message bus.

Database services

All state for the OpenStack web services is stored in a central database, usually a MySQL database. MySQL is usually deployed in an active/passive configuration, but can be made active/active with the Galera replication extension. Galera is clustering software for MySQL (MariaDB in OpenStack) and uses synchronous replication to achieve HA. However, even with Galera, we still recommend directing writes to only one of the replicas; some queries used by the OpenStack services may deadlock when writing to more than one master. With Galera, a load balancer is typically deployed in front of the cluster and is configured to deliver traffic to only one replica at a time. This configuration reduces the mean time to recovery of the service while ensuring that the data is consistent.

In practice, many organizations will defer to database architects for their preference regarding highly available MySQL deployments. After all, it is typically the database administration team who is responsible for responding to failures of that component.

The message bus

All OpenStack services communicate through the message bus. Most OpenStack deployments these days use the RabbitMQ service as the message bus. RabbitMQ can be configured to be active/active through a facility known as **mirrored queues**.

The RabbitMQ service is not load-balanced; each service is given a list of potential nodes and the client is responsible for determining which nodes are active and which ones have failed.

Other messaging services used with OpenStack such as ZeroMQ, ActiveMQ, or Qpid may have different strategies and configurations for achieving HA and horizontal scalability. For these services, refer to the documentation to determine the optimal architecture.

Compute, storage, and network agents

The compute, storage, and network components in OpenStack have a set of services that perform the work that is scheduled by the API services. These services register themselves with the schedulers on startup over the message bus. The schedulers are responsible for determining the health of the services and scheduling work to active services. The compute and storage services are all designed to be run active/active but the network services need some extra consideration.

Each hypervisor in an OpenStack deployment runs the `nova-compute` service. When this service starts up, it registers itself with the `nova-scheduler` service. A list of currently available Nova services is available through the `nova service-list` command. If a compute node is unavailable, its state is listed as down and the scheduler skips it when performing instance actions. When the node becomes available, the scheduler includes it in the list of available hosts.

For KVM or Xen-based deployments, the `nova-compute` service runs once per hypervisor and is not made highly available. For VMware-based deployments though, a single `nova-compute` service is run for every vSphere cluster. As such, this service should be made highly available in an active/passive configuration. This is typically done by virtualizing the service within a vSphere cluster and configuring the virtual machine to be highly available.

Cinder includes a service known as the `volume service` or `cinder-volume`. The volume service registers itself with the Cinder scheduler on startup and is responsible for creating, modifying, or deleting LUNs on block storage devices. For backends that support multiple writers, multiple copies of this service may be run in active/active configuration. The LVM backend (this is the reference backend) is not highly available, though, and may only have one `cinder-volume` service for each block device. This is because the LVM backend is responsible for providing iSCSI access to a locally attached storage device.

For this reason, highly available deployments of OpenStack should avoid the LVM Cinder backend and instead use a backend that supports multiple `cinder-volume` services.

Finally, the Neutron component of OpenStack has a number of agents, which all require some special consideration for highly available deployments. The DHCP agent can be configured as highly available, and the number of agents that will respond to DHCP requests for each subnet is governed by a parameter in the `neutron.conf` file, `dhcp_agents_per_network`. This is typically set to two, regardless of the number of DHCP agents that are configured to run in a control plane.

For most of the history of OpenStack, the L3 routing agent in Neutron has been a single point of failure. This was first addressed by introducing VRRP HA of the L3 agent with the Juno release of OpenStack. With VRRP enabled, the loss of an L3 agent on a controller node no longer interrupts network communication across layer 2 networks. More information on VRRP is available at: `https://docs.openstack.org/newton/networking-guide/deploy-ovs-ha-vrrp.html`. An alternative architecture, called DVR, instead distributes L3 agents out to the compute nodes. Each compute node is attached to the provider network and is responsible for forwarding traffic on behalf of its instances. This is similar to how the `nova-network` service routed packets. More information on DVR is available at: `https://docs.openstack.org/liberty/networking-guide/scenario-dvr-ovs.html`.

Regions, cells, and availability zones

As we mentioned before, OpenStack is designed to be scalable, but not infinitely scalable. There are three different techniques architects can use to segregate an OpenStack cloud: regions, cells, and availability zones. In this section, we'll walk through how each of these concepts maps to hypervisor topologies.

Regions

From an end user's perspective, OpenStack regions are equivalent to regions in Amazon Web Services. Regions live in separate data centers and are often named after their geographical location. If your organization has a data center in Phoenix and one in Raleigh, you'll have at least a PHX and an RDU region. Users who want to geographically disperse their workloads will place some of them in PHX and some of them in RDU. Regions have separate API endpoints, and although the Horizon UI has some support for multiple regions, they are essentially entirely separate deployments.

From an architectural standpoint, there are two main design choices for implementing regions, which are as follows:

- The first is around authorization. Users will want to have the same credentials for accessing each of the OpenStack regions. There are a few ways to accomplish this. The simplest way is to use a common backing store (usually LDAP) for the Keystone service in each region. In this scenario, the user has to authenticate separately to each region to get a token, but the credentials are the same.
- The second major consideration for regional architectures is whether or not to present a single set of Glance images to each region. While work is currently being done to replicate Glance images across federated clouds, most organizations are manually ensuring that the shared images are consistent. This typically involves building a workflow around image publishing and deprecation that is mindful of the regional layout.

Another option for ensuring consistent images across regions is to implement a central image repository using Swift. This also requires shared Keystone and Glance services that span multiple data centers. Details on how to design multiple regions with shared services are in the OpenStack architecture design guide.

Cells

The `nova-compute` service has the concept of **cells**, which can be used to segregate large pools of hypervisors within a single region. This technique is primarily used to mitigate the scalability limits of the OpenStack message bus. The deployment at CERN makes wide use of cells to achieve massive scalability within single regions.

A large amount of work went into the second release of cells (called **cells V2**) in the Ocata release of OpenStack. With cells V2, more services support running in a cell than it did with cells V1, but there are still a number of limitations in Cell-based deployments. Full information on the use of cells is available at: `https://docs.openstack.org/nova/latest/user/cells.html`.

In our experience, it's much simpler to deploy multiple regions within a single data center than to implement cells to achieve large scale. The added inconvenience of presenting your users with multiple API endpoints within a geographic location is typically outweighed by the benefits of having a more robust platform. If multiple control planes are available in a geographic region, the failure of a single control plane becomes less dramatic.

Availability zones

Availability zones are used to group hypervisors within a single OpenStack region. Availability zones are exposed to the end user and should be used to provide the user with an indication of the underlying topology of the cloud. The most common use case for availability zones is to expose failure zones to the user.

To ensure the HA of a service deployed on OpenStack, a user will typically want to deploy the various components of their service onto hypervisors within different racks. This way, the failure of a top of rack switch or a PDU will only bring down a portion of the instances that provide the service. Racks form a natural boundary for availability zones for this reason. There are a few other interesting uses of availability zones apart from exposing failure zones to the end user. One financial services customer we worked with had a requirement for the instances of each line of business to run on dedicated hardware. A combination of availability zones and the `AggregateMultiTenancyIsolation nova-scheduler` filter was used to ensure that each tenant had access to dedicated compute nodes.

Availability zones can also be used to expose hardware classes to end users. For example, hosts with faster processors might be placed in one availability zone and hosts with slower processors might be placed in different availability zones. This allows end users to decide where to place their workloads based upon compute requirements.

Updating the design document

In this chapter, we walked through the different approaches and considerations for achieving HA and scalability in OpenStack deployments. As cloud architects, we need to decide on the correct approach for our deployment and then document it thoroughly so that it can be evaluated by the larger team in our organization.

Each of the major OpenStack vendors have a reference architecture for highly available deployments and these should be used as a starting point for the design. The design should then be integrated with the existing enterprise architecture and modified to ensure that best practices established by the various stakeholders within an organization are followed.

For example, Red Hat's highly available control plane uses the Galera extension to achieve active/active MariaDB services, but the database architects within an organization may only support Oracle's MySQL in an active/passive configuration. The Cloud Architect may choose to implement the database architect's proven pattern instead if they intend on asking for support from the database administration team.

The network architects within an organization may be more comfortable supporting F5 load balancers than HAProxy load balancers.

The system administrators within an organization may be more comfortable supporting Pacemaker than Keepalived. The design document presents the choices made for each of these key technologies and gives the stakeholders an opportunity to comment on them before their deployment.

Planning the physical architecture

In the previous chapter, we updated the *Physical architecture* section to include a definition of the various host groups that we will be deploying. The simplest way to achieve HA is to add additional cloud controllers to the deployment and cluster them. Other deployments may choose to segregate services into different host classes, which can then be clustered. This may include separating the database services into database nodes, separating the messaging services into messaging nodes, and separating the memcached service into memcache nodes.

Load balancing services might live on their own nodes as well. The primary considerations for mapping scalable services to physical (or virtual) hosts are the following:

- Does the service scale horizontally or vertically?
- Will vertically scaling the service impede the performance of other co-located services?
- Does the service have particular hardware or network requirements that other services don't have?

For example, some OpenStack deployments that use the HAProxy load balancing service chose to separate out the load balancing nodes on a separate hardware. The VIPs that the load balancing nodes host must live on a public, routed network, while the internal IPs of services that they route to don't have that requirement. Putting the HAProxy service on separate hosts allows the rest of the control plane to only have private addressing.

Grouping all of the API services on dedicated hosts may simplify horizontal scalability. These services don't need to be managed by a cluster resource manager and can be scaled by adding additional nodes to the load balancers without having to update cluster definitions. Database services have high I/O requirements. Segregating these services onto machines that have access to a high-performance fiber channel may make sense.

Finally, you should consider whether or not to virtualize the control plane. If the control plane will be virtualized, creating additional host groups to host dedicated services becomes very attractive. Having eight or nine virtual machines dedicated to the control plane is a very different proposition from having eight or nine physical machines dedicated to the control plane.

Most highly available control planes require at least three nodes to ensure that a quorum is easily determined by the cluster resource manager. While dedicating three physical nodes to the control function of a hundred-node OpenStack deployment makes a lot of sense, dedicating nine physical nodes may not. Many of the organizations that we've worked with will already have a VMware-based cluster available for hosting management appliances and the control plane can be deployed within that existing footprint. Organizations that are deploying a KVM-only cloud may not want to incur the additional operational complexity of managing the additional virtual machines outside OpenStack.

Updating the physical architecture design

Once the mapping of services to physical (or virtual) machines has been determined, the design document should be updated to include a definition of the host groups and their associated functions. A simple example is provided as follows:

- **Load balancer**: These systems provide the load balancing services in an active/passive configuration
- **Cloud controller**: These systems provide the API services, the scheduling services, and the Horizon dashboard services in an active/active configuration
- **Database node**: These systems provide the MySQL database services in an active/passive configuration
- **Messaging node**: These systems provide the RabbitMQ messaging services in an active/active configuration
- **Compute node**: These systems act as KVM hypervisors and run the `nova-compute` and `openvswitch-agent` services

Deployments that will be using only the cloud controller host group might use the following definitions:

- **Cloud controller**: These systems provide the load balancing services in an active/passive configuration and the API services, MySQL database services, and RabbitMQ messaging services in an active/active configuration
- **Compute node**: These systems act as KVM hypervisors and run the `nova-compute` and `openvswitch-agent` services

After defining the host groups, the physical architecture diagram should be updated to reflect the mapping of host groups to physical machines in the deployment. This should also include considerations for network connectivity. The following is an example architecture diagram for inclusion in the design document:

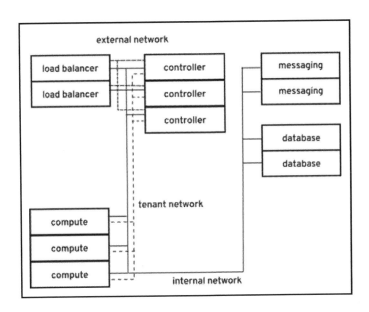

Implementing HA in the lab deployment

In this last section, we'll make the current lab deployment that we deployed in Chapter 2, *Architecting the Cloud*, highly available by adding a second controller node and configuring cluster software. This example should be simple enough to easily implement in the lab, while still allowing you to evaluate the technology.

Provisioning a second controller

In later chapters, we'll look at more flexible deployment methodologies that allow fine-grained service placement and automated cluster configuration. In this chapter, we'll just extend the Packstack deployment from Chapter 2, *Architecting the Cloud*. Packstack isn't designed to deploy multiple controllers, so some manual configuration of services will be required.

To provision the second controller, install the operating system on a new machine in the same way you provisioned the first controller and then copy the Packstack answer file from the first controller. Edit the answer and replace CONFIG_CONTROLLER_HOST, CONFIG_NETWORK_HOSTS, and CONFIG_STORAGE_HOST with the IP address of the new controller.

We won't be reconfiguring the compute nodes or the existing controller, so add the compute nodes and controller that you provisioned in Chapter 2, *Architecting the Cloud*, to the EXCLUDE_SERVERS parameter in the answer file. We'll leave the MySQL, Redis, MongoDB, and RabbitMQ services on the first controller, so those values should not be modified.

Run Packstack on the new controller using the same command we used in Chapter 2, *Architecting the Cloud*:

```
packstack --answer-file <answer-file>
```

After Packstack completes, you should be able to log in to the dashboard by going to the IP address of the second host and using the same credentials that you used in Chapter 2, *Architecting the Cloud*.

Installing the Pacemaker resource manager

Next, we'll install Pacemaker to manage the VIPs that we'll use with HAProxy to make the web services highly available. We assume that the cluster software is already available through yum to the controller nodes.

1. First, install Pacemaker on both nodes using the following command:

   ```
   # yum install -y pcs fence-agents-all
   ```

2. Verify that the software is installed correctly by running the following command:

   ```
   # rpm -q pcs
   pcs-0.9.137-13.el7_1.3.x86_64
   ```

3. Next, add rules to the firewall to allow cluster traffic:

   ```
   # firewall-cmd --permanent --add-service=high-availability
   ```

4. Set the password for the Pacemaker cluster on each node using the following command:

   ```
   # passwd hacluster
   ```

5. Start the Pacemaker cluster manager on each node:

```
# systemctl start pcsd.service
# systemctl enable pcsd.service
```

6. Then, authenticate the nodes using the following commands on the first node:

```
# pcs cluster auth controller1 controller2 Username: hacluster
Password:
controller1: Authorized controller2: Authorized
```

7. Finally, run the following commands on the first node to create the cluster and start it:

```
# pcs cluster setup --start --name openstack \
> controller1 controller2
Shutting down pacemaker/corosync services... Redirecting to
/bin/systemctl stop    pacemaker.service Redirecting to
/bin/systemctl stop    corosync.service Killing any remaining
services...
Removing all cluster configuration files... controller1: Succeeded
controller2: Succeeded
Starting cluster on nodes: controller1, controller2... controller1:
Starting Cluster...
controller2: Starting Cluster...
```

8. For our example cluster, we will disable fencing using the following command:

```
# pcs property set stonith-enabled=false
```

9. Verify that the cluster started successfully using the following command:

```
# pcs status
Cluster name: openstack
Last updated: Mon Aug 31 01:51:47 2015
Last change: Mon Aug 31 01:51:14 2015 Stack: corosync
Current DC: controller1 (1) - partition with quorum Version:
1.1.12-a14efad
2 Nodes configured
0 Resources configured
Online: [ controller1 controller2 ]
```

For more information on setting up Pacemaker, see the excellent clusters from scratch documentation at: http://clusterlabs.org/pacemaker/doc/en-US/Pacemaker/1.1/html/ Clusters_from_Scratch/.

Installing and configuring HAProxy

We'll be using HAProxy to load balance our control plane services in this lab deployment. Some deployments may also implement Keepalived and run HAProxy in an active/active configuration. For this deployment, we'll run HAProxy active/passive and manage it as a resource along with our VIP in Pacemaker.

To start, install HAProxy on both nodes using the following command:

```
# yum -y install haproxy
```

Verify the installation with the following command:

```
# rpm -q haproxy
haproxy-1.5.4-4.el7_1.x86_64
```

Next, we will create a configuration file for HAProxy that load balances the API services installed on the two controllers. Use the following example as a template, replacing the IP addresses in the example with the IP addresses of the two controllers and the IP address of the VIP that you'll be using to load balance the API services.

The following example, /etc/haproxy/haproxy.cfg, will load balance Horizon in our environment:

```
global
  daemon
  group    haproxy
  maxconn  40000
  pidfile  /var/run/haproxy.pid
  user     haproxy

defaults
  log 127.0.0.1 local2 warning
  mode    tcp
  option tcplog
  option redispatch
  retries      3
  timeout    connect 10s
   timeout    client 60s
   timeout    server 60s
   timeout    check 10s

listen horizon
  bind 192.168.0.30:80
  mode http
  cookie SERVERID insert indirect nocache
```

```
option tcplog
timeout client 180s
server controller1 192.168.0.10:80 cookie controller1 check inter 1s
server controller2 192.168.0.11:80 cookie controller2 check inter 1s
```

In this example, controller1 has an IP address of `192.168.0.10` and `controller2` has an IP address of `192.168.0.11`. The VIP that we've chosen to use is `192.168.1.30`. Update the file, replacing the IP addresses with the addresses in your lab, in `/etc/haproxy/haproxy.cfg` on each of the controllers.

In order for Horizon to respond to requests on the VIP, we'll need to add the VIP as a `ServerAlias` in the Apache virtual host configuration. This is found at `/etc/httpd/conf.d/15-horizon_vhost.conf` in our lab installation. Look for the following line:

```
ServerAlias 192.168.0.10
```

Add an additional `ServerAlias` line with the VIP on both controllers:

```
ServerAlias 192.168.0.30
```

You'll also need to tell Apache not to listen on the VIP so that HAProxy can bind to the address. To do this, modify `/etc/httpd/conf/ports.conf` and specify the IP address of the controller in addition to the port numbers. The following is an example:

```
Listen 192.168.0.10:35357
Listen 192.168.0.10:5000
Listen 192.168.0.10:80
```

In this example, `192.168.0.10` is the address of the first controller. Substitute the appropriate IP address for each machine.

Restart Apache to pick up the new alias:

```
# systemctl restart httpd.service
```

Next, add the VIP and the HAProxy service to the Pacemaker cluster as resources. These commands should only be run on the first node:

```
# pcs resource create VirtualIP IPaddr2 ip=192.168.0.30 cidr_netmask=24
# pcs resource create HAProxy systemd:haproxy
```

Co-locate the HAProxy service with the `VirtualIP` to ensure that the two run together:

```
# pcs constraint colocation add VirtualIP with HAProxy score=INFINITY
```

Verify that the resources have been started:

```
# pcs status
...
Full list of resources: VirtualIP(ocf::heartbeat:IPaddr2):Started
controller1 HAProxy(systemd:haproxy):Started controller1
...
```

At this point, you should be able to access Horizon using the VIP you specified. Traffic will flow from your client to HAProxy on the VIP to Apache on one of the two nodes.

Additional API service configuration

Now that we have a working cluster and HAProxy configuration, the final configuration step is to move each of the OpenStack API endpoints behind the load balancer. There are three steps in this process, which are as follows:

1. Update the HAProxy configuration to include the service
2. Move the endpoint in the Keystone service catalog to the VIP
3. Reconfigure the services to point to the VIP instead of the IP of the first controller

In the following example, we will move the Keystone service behind the load balancer. This process can be followed for each of the API services.

First, add a section to the HAProxy configuration file for the authorization and admin endpoints of Keystone:

```
listen keystone-admin
  bind 192.168.0.30:35357
  mode tcp option tcplog
  server controller1 192.168.0.10:35357 check inter 1s
  server   controller2 192.168.0.11:35357 check inter 1s

listen keystone-public
  bind 192.168.0.30:5000
  mode tcp option tcplog
  server controller1 192.168.0.10:5000 check inter 1s
  server controller2 192.168.0.11:5000 check inter 1s
```

Make sure to update the configuration on both of the controllers. Restart the HAproxy service on the active node:

```
# systemctl restart haproxy.service
```

You can determine the active node with the output from `pcs status`. Check to make sure that HAProxy is now listening on ports 5000 and 35357 using the following commands:

```
# curl http://192.168.0.30:5000
# curl http://192.168.0.30:35357
```

Both should output some JSON describing the status of the Keystone service.

Next, update the endpoint for the identity service in the Keystone service catalog by creating a new endpoint and deleting the old one:

```
# . ./keystonerc_admin
# openstack endpoint list
+-------------------------------+-----------+--------------+--------
------+
| ID   | Region | Service Name | Service Type |
+-------------------------------+-----------+--------------+--------
------+
| 14f32353dd7d497d9816bf0302279d23 | RegionOne | keystone   | identity |
...
# openstack endpoint create \
--adminurl http://192.168.0.30:35357/v2.0 \
--internalurl http://192.168.0.30:5000/v2.0 \
--publicurl http://192.168.0.30:5000/v2.0 \
--region RegionOne keystone
+--------------+------------------------------------+
| Field   | Value  |
+--------------+------------------------------------+
| adminurl   | http://192.168.0.30:35357/v2.0 |
| id   | c590765ca1a847db8b79aa5f40cd2110 |
...
# openstack endpoint delete 14f32353dd7d497d9816bf0302279d23
```

Lastly, update the `auth_uri` and `identity_uri` parameters in each of the OpenStack services to point to the new IP address. The following configuration files will need to be edited:

- /etc/ceilometer/ceilometer.conf
- /etc/cinder/api-paste.ini
- /etc/glance/glance-api.conf
- /etc/glance/glance-registry.conf
- /etc/neutron/neutron.conf
- /etc/neutron/api-paste.ini
- /etc/nova/nova.conf

- `/etc/swift/proxy-server.conf`

After editing each of the files, restart the OpenStack services on all of the nodes in the lab deployment using the following command:

```
# openstack-service restart
```

The OpenStack services will now be using the Keystone API endpoint provided by the VIP and the service will be highly available. The architecture used in this cluster is relatively simple, but it provides an example of both active/active and active/passive service configurations.

Summary

A complete guide to implementing HA for OpenStack services is probably worth a book of its own. In this chapter, we started out by covering the main strategies for making OpenStack services highly available and identifying which strategies apply well to each service. Then, we covered how OpenStack deployments are typically segmented across physical regions. Finally, we updated our documentation and implemented a few of the technologies we discussed in the lab.

While walking through the main considerations for highly available deployments in this chapter, we've tried to emphasize a few key points:

- Scalability is at least as important as HA in cluster design
- Ensure that your design is flexible in case of unexpected growth
- OpenStack doesn't scale forever. Plan for multiple regions

Also, it's important to make sure that the strategy and architecture that you adopt for HA are supportable by your organization. Consider reusing existing architectures for HA in the message bus and database layers.

Further reading

Please refer to the following links for further reading:

- **The OpenStack architecture design guide**: `http://docs.openstack.org/arch-design/content/index.html`
- **Clusters from scratch**: `http://clusterlabs.org/doc/en-US/Pacemaker/1.1/html/Clusters_from_Scratch/`

4
Building the Deployment Pipeline

We often tell customers that we work with OpenStack. However, it is not installed but deployed. Although the difference in words might seem subtle, it can really be a revolutionary change within an organization. Most enterprise infrastructure teams are used to the following process in the deployment of a new infrastructure platform:

1. Installing the platform
2. Configuring and integrating the platform
3. Running the platform
4. Upgrading the platform

Installing and configuring the platform can take months or years, and once it's installed, the platform is expected to run for years. Upgrades to the platform happen every 3 to 5 years, and they are large 6-12 month projects. Red Hat has structured the release of our Enterprise Linux operating system around these cycles—there were 3 years between the release of RHEL 5 and RHEL 6 and almost 4 years between RHEL 6 and RHEL 7. Each release is supported for 10 years, and conservative infrastructure teams will wait at least a year after the release of a new version to start their 6-12 month upgrade project.

This kind of conservative approach to platform deployment has worked extremely well in the operating system, virtualization platform, and application platform spaces. However, if the most important business driver for your private cloud project is increased agility, you are unlikely to achieve your goal with a 12-month roll-out and a 5-year life cycle.

In this chapter, we'll be looking at how OpenStack is deployed as an application software, not as an infrastructure software. We'll build a simple deployment pipeline that uses Puppet to describe an OpenStack deployment, uses Jenkins as an open source **Continuous Integration (CI)** tool to realize that deployment, and then runs unit tests to verify that the deployment meets our specifications. Throughout the chapter, we'll talk about iterative development and how it applies to OpenStack deployments.

In this chapter, we will cover the following topics:

- Dealing with Infrastructure as a Software
- Using configuration management for deployment
- Test infrastructure
- Creating the composition layer
- Installing Keystone

Dealing with Infrastructure as a Software

A Vice President of Infrastructure at a large company once told us something like this, *I like hardware. My hardware hardly ever breaks. The software I deploy breaks all the time. When my data center becomes software, how will I ever have a stable platform?* Although the same concern could (and probably should) have once been applied to virtualization, most organizations today are very comfortable with the idea of software pretending to be hardware. The software-defined data center is something a little more intimidating though. Although we've had software pretending to be a CPU for a long time, we've only had software pretending to be a storage array relatively recently. Also, when the storage array goes down, everything tends to come down with it.

However, maybe the bigger question is around software constantly breaking on deployment. Indeed, the most successful OpenStack deployments that we've worked with have all adopted modern software development techniques to ensure that their software does not break on deployment.

Eating the elephant

The first and most important concept that we will apply to our deployment process is that of iterative development. Instead of trying to tackle all the requirements that we've identified in one deployment, we break it down into stories, assign them to 2-or 3-week sprints, and then implement them one by one. A sprint is a basic measure of development derived from the Scrum process and framework. A sprint is a timeboxed measure of effort that is planned and limited to a specific duration (2 weeks is common). Not only does this allow us to limit the complexity of each release and focus on thoroughly testing each component, but it also allows us to begin returning value to the business much sooner in the process. Workloads that only require a small feature set will be able to board the platform without waiting for a large release.

Writing the tests first

The second most important practice that we will pull from the software development world is that of test-driven development. We write the test that demonstrates the functionality we're implementing first and then work on the deployment until the test passes. Once the feature has been implemented, the test then becomes part of the routine monitoring system for the platform.

In our experience, if the tests aren't written before the code, they are frequently not written. Every project runs out of time at some point, and if the tests are the last thing on the list, they tend to get cut.

Always be deploying

The benefits of continuous deployment have been well described for some time in the software development world, but they're particularly applicable to OpenStack deployments. Lots of small, well-tested changes tend to cause much less disruption to a complex environment such as a private cloud deployment than a few, huge well-tested changes.

There are some exceptions to this, though. For example, moving from Nova Networking to Neutron is a major change that cannot easily be broken up into smaller pieces. Adding a new Cinder driver is a small iterative change, but changing from one Cinder driver to another can be a massive change in environments with large numbers of volumes to migrate. Care should be taken when making architectural decisions to try to avoid large changes to the platform that cannot be iteratively developed and deployed.

Using configuration management for deployment

The first tool required to begin deploying our platform-like code is to introduce a configuration management system. Although it is certainly possible to automate the deployment of OpenStack using shell scripts (we've seen it done), using a declarative configuration management tool makes it much more simple for your team to track changes between iterations.

Also, an OpenStack configuration can contain hundreds of variables that need to be set across several configuration files on dozens of hosts. For example, our lab deployment of OpenStack has 137 parameters set in the composition layer. Managing this level of complexity with shell scripts introduces another unnecessary level of complexity.

Every OpenStack user survey for the past couple of years has asked the community how they typically deploy OpenStack. Although a wide variety of methods are represented in the results, the clear leader has been Puppet for some time now. A new initiative in the community has grown up around Ansible in the past year, and its use has increased dramatically. A few prominent OpenStack users also use Chef for deployment. Our recommendation is to use the tool that your organization has the most experience with. Some of the groups that we've worked with already had large implementations of Puppet, some of them had expertise in Chef, and some prefer to use Ansible. We've also worked on projects that leveraged Salt. A new trend that is emerging is to use a combination of tools. You might have Ansible or Salt initiate Puppet running on your hosts, for example. Puppet is the most frequently used, and we'll use it in the examples in this chapter.

Using the community modules

Each of the configuration management systems referenced earlier has a set of modules for deploying OpenStack that are written and maintained by the OpenStack community. For example, consider the following table:

Orchestration tool's OpenStack modules	Location
Puppet modules	`https://wiki.openstack.org/wiki/Puppet`
Ansible playbooks	`https://wiki.openstack.org/wiki/OpenStackAnsible`
Chef cookbooks	`https://wiki.openstack.org/wiki/Chef`

Regardless of the technology used, the overall approach is the same.

A deployment starts with the creation of what we'll refer to as the composition layer. This is a Puppet module (or Ansible playbook or Chef cookbook) that defines the roles we want the systems in our deployment to take in terms of the community modules. For example, we might define a compute role as a class, which would include the `nova::compute` class. The controller role would include the keystone, glance, `nova::api`, and other classes. We may also pull in other Puppet modules to configure system services such as NTP or to install monitoring agents.

Assigning roles

Once we've declared our roles in the composition layer, we need a mechanism via which we apply them to systems. The tool that we've been using up to this point (Packstack) does this over SSH—it generates a set of Puppet manifests that include the community modules and then it applies them to the systems in our lab one by one. It supports two roles: the controller role and the compute role. Our lab deployment currently has controller and compute nodes, but we'll also be defining database nodes that can run the database and messaging services.

Many of the organizations that we've worked with have used Cobbler (`http://cobbler.github.io`), Foreman (`http://theforeman.org`), Puppet Enterprise (`https://puppetlabs.com/puppet/puppet-enterprise`), or some other tool to assign roles to systems. These tools are referred to as **External Node Classifiers (ENC)** for Puppet. With ENC, it's easy to separate the configuration parameters, such as IP addresses or passwords, from the configuration itself in the system. These tools can also provide reporting on Puppet runs and management functionality.

In this chapter, we'll set up a simple Puppet master that will manage the configuration of the hosts in our environment. We'll store configuration data in our composition layer, acknowledging that it's not a best practice.

We'll assign the roles we've defined to the hosts on the Puppet master, and when hosts check in with the master, they'll be given the configuration that matches their role. Hosts check in periodically after the first run and will pull updates to the configuration as we make them available on the master.

Choosing a starting point

Each of the official OpenStack Puppet, Chef, and Ansible projects listed earlier provide example composition layers which will do a simple all-in-one deployment. The Puppet all-in-one deployment manifest is available at `https://github.com/openstack/puppet-openstack-integration`. It provides three scenarios, which can be used as a starting point. Different OpenStack vendors may also have references that make good starting points. Some organizations we've worked with have hired consulting firms to write their initial composition layer and then teach them how to iterate on it.

Since we already have a working deployment using Packstack, we'll use that as a basis for our composition layer. As we add features to our deployment, we'll copy in pieces from the manifests generated by Packstack as a starting point. We'll also add some new Puppet code to extend the deployment beyond what's possible with Packstack.

Test infrastructure

Regardless of the configuration management system that your organization decides to use to deploy and configure the OpenStack software, it is critical that the deployment process is driven by the test infrastructure. It has been our experience that manually administrated environments always result in inconsistency, regardless of the skill of the operator performing the deployment. Automated deployments cannot happen in a vacuum however, for them to be successful, they need to provide immediate feedback to the developer and operator so that they can decide whether the deployment was successful. We've been through a lot of manual deployments and manual acceptance tests using OpenStack, and the cycles can take days or weeks to complete.

Types of testing

There are several stages of testing that are applied to the changes in the composition layer before they're applied to the environment. At each stage, the deployment is stopped if the tests fail. We refer to this set of stages as the deployment pipeline. Changes are committed to version control on one end of the pipeline, and the configuration is realized in the infrastructure on the other end.

The following table lists the items that are tested at each stage in the pipeline:

Stage	Test focus
Precommit	Before the change enters the pipeline, it is tested to ensure that there are no syntax errors or style issues.
Deployment testing	At this stage, each of the systems in the test cluster attempts to apply the configuration update. Success is indicated by whether the change is applied without errors. Some deployments will initiate a second application to test for idempotency.
Integration testing	Once the test cluster has successfully applied the configuration, a unit test suite is run against the OpenStack APIs, verifying the functionality of the configuration.

Performance testing	A series of tests are run against the test cluster to ensure that the change did not adversely affect performance.
Acceptance testing	At this stage in the pipeline, any manual testing is performed. The change is then promoted to the next environment.
Canary testing	A subset of the production environment is updated with the change and automated, and the acceptance testing is repeated with the production database and hypervisors.
Release	The entire production environment is updated with the change.

Many organizations will want to include a code review in the deployment process. This is typically done after all automated testing is complete so that the results are available to the reviewer. Tools such as Gerrit (https://www.gerritcodereview.com/) are available to orchestrate build pipelines that have code review requirements. Many organizations will prefer to perform canary testing and production releases manually—these should still be automated processes that are initiated (and rolled back) at the discretion of operators.

Writing the tests

OpenStack is entirely driven by the REST API, and it is possible to write tests for the platform in any language that has an HTTP client implementation. There are software development kits available at http://developer.openstack.org for most popular languages. That said, most organizations tend to write their tests in Python (the language OpenStack is written in). There are two schools of thought on this. The first is that it is easier to attract OpenStack talent who know Python, and the skill is transferable between testing and development. Also, there is an upstream Python project named **Tempest**, which many organizations use as a framework for running their own tests. The second school of thought is that organizations should test the platform using the same interface that end users of the platform will use. For example, if your intention is for the infrastructure to be provisioned from a Cloud Management Platform or a PaaS using the Ruby Fog library (http://fog.io/), then your tests should be written using the Fog library.

Either way, Tempest is almost always used in some part of the testing process for OpenStack deployments. If nothing else, all public clouds that advertise themselves as OpenStack clouds must pass a minimum set of Tempest tests to achieve certification with the Foundation.

Running the tests

As we mentioned earlier, the test infrastructure should drive the changes through the pipeline, capturing the results of each test run and promoting changes when the runs are successful. Any of the many CI tools used for software development can be used for this purpose. What we typically recommend is to leverage the CI tools and software repositories that your organization is already using. If your organization isn't doing CI in your software development group, good choices that we've seen used successfully before are Jenkins (`https://jenkins-ci.org/`), Atlassian's Bamboo (`https://www.atlassian.com/software/bamboo/`), or Buildbot (`http://buildbot.net/`). The OpenStack Foundation's CI is built around Jenkins, and it's the tool that we'll use in this chapter to build our pipeline.

Putting the pipeline together

Now that we've described the different components of the deployment pipeline, let's assemble an example pipeline in our lab environment. We'll start by setting up the CI server, creating a new composition layer, writing a unit test, and then deploying the OpenStack infrastructure to pass the test.

Setting up the CI server

In previous chapters, we deployed OpenStack by running the `packstack` utility from the cloud controller. In this section, we'll be setting up a dedicated machine to do our deployments. The requirements for our deployment machine are not too strenuous—any machine running CentOS 7 with 2 GB of RAM or more should suffice. The only network requirements are that the machine is reachable from both the intranet and from the OpenStack cluster itself.

Installing Git

The following instructions will set up a Git version control server on the CI server. If you already have access to a Git repository or prefer to use GitHub, you can skip this section. For more information on setting up a Git server, refer to the *Pro Git* book by Scott Chacon and Ben Straub, available on the internet at `https://git-scm.com/book/en/v2/`.

To install the Apache HTTP server and the Git version control software, execute the following steps:

1. Execute the following command as a root on the CI server:

   ```
   # yum install -y httpd git
   ```

2. Verify that the packages were correctly installed:

   ```
   # rpm -q httpd git
   ```

3. Create a top-level directory to hold our repository:

   ```
   # mkdir /var/www/html/git
   ```

4. Create the Git repository in the directory with the following commands:

   ```
   # mkdir /var/www/html/git/openstack/
   # cd /var/www/html/git/openstack
   # git --bare init
   # git update-server-info
   ```

5. You should see the following response after the `git --bare init` command:

   ```
   Initialized empty Git repository in /var/www/git/openstack/
   ```

6. Reset permissions on the new Git repository for Apache:

   ```
   # chown -R apache:apache /var/www/html/git/
   ```

7. Finally, create a configuration file that requires authentication for the Git repository. The following example can be copied to `/etc/httpd/conf.d/git.conf`:

   ```
   <Directory /var/www/html/git/>
     DAV on

     AuthName "Git login:"
     AuthType Basic
     AuthUserFile   /var/www/htpasswd

     # Allow anonymous clone, but require auth for push.
     <LimitExcept GET PROPFIND>
       Require valid-user
     </LimitExcept>
   </Directory>
   ```

8. Create a user account for us to use for the repository:

   ```
   # htpasswd -c /var/www/htpasswd git
   ```

9. Last, restart the httpd server:

   ```
   # systemctl restart httpd
   ```

   You should now be able to clone the Git repository using the following command:

   ```
   # git clone http://git@localhost/git/openstack
   ```

   You may be prompted for the password that you entered when creating the user account, and you should receive the following message:

   ```
   warning: You appear to have cloned an empty repository.
   ```

Installing a Puppet master

The following instructions will set up a Puppet master on the CI server. If you already have a Puppet infrastructure that you can use in your laboratory, you can skip this section. For more information on setting up a Puppet master, refer to the Puppet Reference Manual (http://docs.puppetlabs.com/puppet/latest/reference/). Install the RDO repository, which provides access to both the Puppet and the OpenStack Puppet modules using the following steps:

1. Execute the following command as root on the CI server:

   ```
   # yum install -y https://rdoproject.org/repos/rdo-release.rpm
   ```

2. Verify that the repository has been enabled by running the following command:

   ```
   # yum repolist
   ```

3. You should see the OpenStack repository in the output. Run the following command to install Puppet and the OpenStack Puppet modules:

   ```
   # yum install -y puppet puppet-server openstack-packstack
   ```

4. Verify their installation with the following command:

   ```
   # rpm -q puppet puppet-server openstack-packstack
   ```

5. Edit the Puppet configuration to include the OpenStack Puppet modules:

```
# puppet config set basemodulepath \
'$confdir/modules:/usr/share/puppet/modules:/usr/share/openstack-
puppet/modules' \
--section main
```

6. Verify the configuration by listing the available Puppet modules:

```
# puppet module list
```

   You should see around 60 Puppet modules, depending on the version of OpenStack. Ignore any errors about dependencies.

7. Start the Puppet master service using the following command:

```
# systemctl start puppetmaster.service
# systemctl enable puppetmaster.service
```

8. Verify that the service started correctly:

```
# systemctl status puppetmaster.service -l
```

You should see that the service has created a certificate authority. It is important that the clients in your environment access the Puppet master using the same hostname as the certificate authority. If the clients will be accessing the Puppet master over more than the hostname, look into using the dns_alt_names setting for puppet.conf.

Installing Jenkins

The following instructions will set up a Jenkins server on the CI server. If you already have a Jenkins server that you can use in your lab, you can skip this section. For more information on setting up Jenkins, refer to the Jenkins website (https://wiki.jenkins-ci. org/display/JENKINS/Use+Jenkins):

1. Execute the following commands as root on the CI server to install the Jenkins repository, which provides access to Jenkins:

```
# curl http://pkg.jenkins-ci.org/redhat/jenkins.repo >
/etc/yum.repos.d/jenkins.repo
# rpm --import https://jenkins-ci.org/redhat/jenkins-ci.org.key
# yum install -y java-1.8.0-openjdk jenkins
```

2. To verify that the software was installed correctly, run the following command:

```
# rpm -q java-1.8.0-openjdk jenkins
```

3. To start the jenkins server, use the following command:

```
# systemctl start jenkins
```

4. Verify that Jenkins started correctly using the following command:

```
# systemctl status jenkins -l
```

You should see that the service is running and that there are no errors in the log output.

5. You can now log in to the Jenkins web UI by visiting your host on port 8080 in your web browser; that is, if your CI server's hostname is jenkins.example.com, Jenkins should be available at http://jenkins.example.com:8080/. Newer installations of Jenkins will prompt you to enter a code from the local filesystem before you log in:

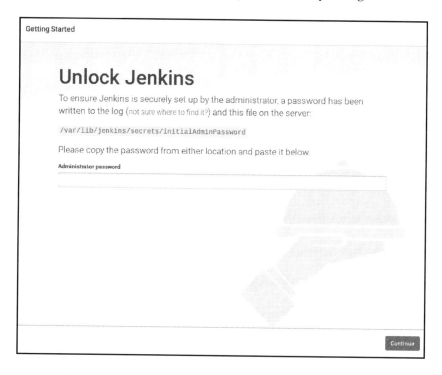

6. Next, you will be prompted to install the default set of plugins that users typically configure. Select **Install suggested plugins**:

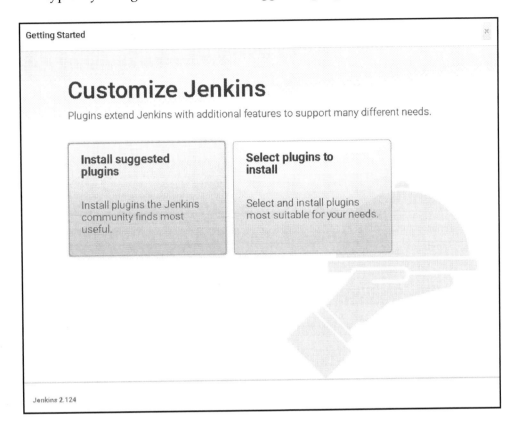

You'll see the status of the installation as it progresses. When it completes successfully, you'll be prompted to create an administrative user:

Jenkins is now installed and configured with the Git plugin.

Creating the composition layer

Now that our infrastructure software is in place, we'll begin creating our composition layer. As we mentioned earlier, we'll be starting with the *known good* configuration we got from running the Packstack command in `Chapter 2`, *Architecting the Cloud*.

Starting our Puppet modules

Our composition layer will be stored in two Puppet modules, using the **profiles and roles** pattern developed by Craig Dunn (http://www.craigdunn.org/2012/05/239/). We'll store the modules in a directory named puppet/modules in our new Git repository. The following steps will create the new modules within our repository:

1. Clone the repository. It is recommended to use an unprivileged user account for this section:

    ```
    $ git clone http://git@localhost/git/openstack/
    ```

2. Next, create the directory for the modules:

    ```
    $ mkdir -p openstack/puppet/modules
    ```

3. Use the puppet/modules command to create the new modules in the directory:

    ```
    $ cd openstack/puppet/modules
    $ puppet module generate openstack-profile
    $ puppet module generate openstack-role
    ```

    For each of these commands, you will be prompted for a set of metadata about the module. Enter as much information as you'd like or use the defaults.

4. Once you've set up the modules as you like, go back to the top level of the code repository and check them into revision control with the following commands:

    ```
    $ cd ~/openstack
    $ git add puppet
    $ git commit -m 'Initial check-in of the profile and role modules'
    $ git push origin master
    ```

    You should see that the modules have been committed and pushed into a new master branch on the repository.

5. Now, let's add these modules to our Puppet master. To do this, clone a clean copy of the repository onto a location on the server as the root user:

    ```
    # cd /srv
    # git clone http://localhost/git/openstack
    ```

    You should receive a message such as Cloning into openstack..., which will indicate the success of the command.

6. We'll be updating this repository with a Jenkins job, so change the ownership of the directory to the Jenkins user:

```
# chown -R jenkins:jenkins /srv/openstack
```

If you're using a remote Jenkins server, you'll need to set permissions so that you can log in to this machine remotely and run the git pull command in that directory.

7. Next, symlink the two new Puppet modules into /etc/puppet/modules on the master:

```
# cd /etc/puppet/modules
# ln -s /srv/openstack/puppet/modules/profile profile
# ln -s /srv/openstack/puppet/modules/role role
```

You should now see the two modules in the output of the Puppet module list on the master:

```
/etc/puppet/modules
├──    openstack-profile (v0.1.0)
└──    openstack-role (v0.1.0)
```

Defining the first role and profile

We already have a set of host groups defined in our design document. We'll map these directly to roles in our Puppet composition layer. Each role will get its own class and file in the role Puppet module. A role comprises profiles, each of which represents a piece of OpenStack functionality. For example, the Mariadb profile will install and configure the MySQL database server for our deployment, the amqp profile will install and configure the RabbitMQ message server, and so on. Let's start by creating a Database Node role and associated profile.

As we mentioned earlier, we'll use the Packstack configuration that we created in Chapter 2, *Architecting the Cloud*, as a starting point for our composition layer. Normally, when Packstack runs, it deletes the Puppet manifests that it uses to install the OpenStack software on the hosts. However, If you specify the -y option, it will exit without doing anything and leave the Puppet manifests in place. On the original host that you ran Packstack on Chapter 2, *Architecting the Cloud*, rerun Packstack with the same answer file and the -y option:

```
# packstack --answer-file=packstack.answers -y
```

After the command has completed execution, it will print the name of the directory where it wrote the Puppet manifests. It should be something like `/var/tmp/packstack/20151113-214424-gIbMJA`. Descend into that directory and copy the Hiera data and manifests to your CI server.

Packstack's Puppet manifests use Hiera, Puppet's key/value lookup tool, to make it easy to store configuration information such as passwords and IP addresses so that they don't need to be stored in the manifests themselves. We'll stay with this practice. Copy the hieradata directory to `/etc/puppet/hieradata` on the CI server. To tell Puppet to reference this data and create a file named `/etc/puppet/hiera.yaml` with the following contents:

```
---
:backends:
  - yaml
:hierarchy:
  - defaults
  - "%{clientcert}"
  - "%{environment}"
  - global

:yaml:
  :datadir: /etc/puppet/hieradata
```

Now, let's create the first profile. Create a new file named `puppet/modules/profile/manifests/mariadb.pp` in our checked-out copy of the OpenStack repository. Once again, use an unprivileged account.

Starting with the Newton release of RDO, the manifests created by the Packstack tool have adopted the roles and profiles model that we're implementing in this chapter. Two roles exist in Packstack—one for controllers and one for compute nodes. We'll be creating a new role by copying relevant profiles from the controller manifest. In `mariadb.pp`, create a class definition as follows:

```
class profile::mariadb {
  include '::packstack::mariadb'
  include '::packstack::mariadb::services'
}
```

This defines the Mariadb profile with the same Puppet code that we used to install the database in our Packstack installation. Now create a file named `puppet/modules/role/manifests/database.pp`. Create a class named `role::database` in that file, which references the profile we created earlier:

```
class role::database {
  include profile::mariadb
}
```

Add the two files to a commit and then commit and push them to the Git server.

Running the first build

Visit Jenkins at `http://jenkins:8080/`, replacing jenkins with the hostname of your CI server. The Jenkins UI should come up, prompting you to create a new job.

Click on **create new jobs**:

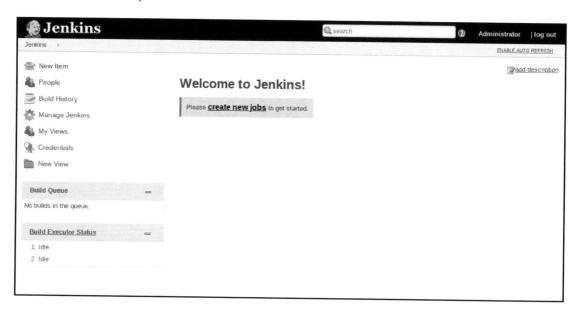

Create a new freestyle project named `openstack`, as shown here:

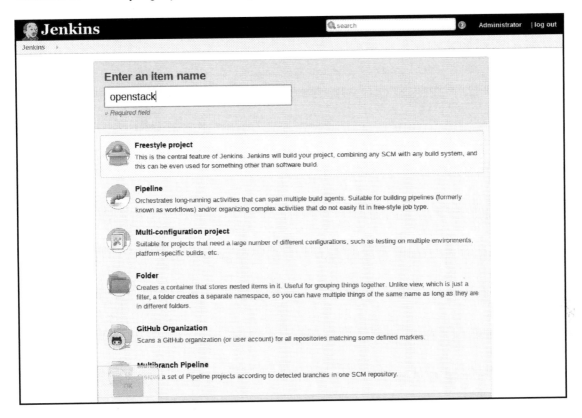

Now, we'll specify the options for the project. First, under **Source Code Management**, select **Git** and specify `http://localhost/git/openstack` for your repository. (This assumes that you're using the Git server that we set up on the CI server. If you're using a remote Git repository, enter the clone URL for that instead.):

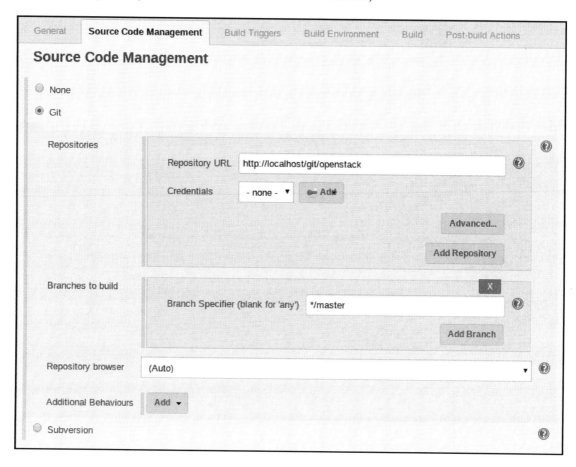

Next, we'll add a step to update the Puppet master with the latest code from the repository. Under **Build**, click on **Add build step** and select **Execute shell**. Specify the following command:

```
cd /srv/openstack && git fetch
cd /srv/openstack && git checkout -f $GIT_COMMIT
```

This will update the copy of the repository that the Puppet master pulls from the version we're testing:

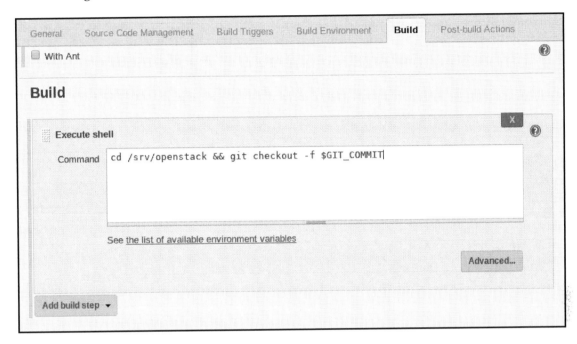

Let's run a build to make sure that permissions are set correctly. Save the project. This will bring you back to the project page. Select **Build Now**. You'll see your first build in the **Build History** tab on the bottom left.

Clicking on the build number will present you with information as to whether the build succeeded or failed and allow you to view the console output of the build.

To verify that Jenkins pulled our new changes into the modules, look for the new files in `/etc/puppet/modules`:

```
# ls /etc/puppet/modules/profile/manifests/
# ls /etc/puppet/modules/role/manifests/
```

You should see the Mariadb profile and the database role files in these directories.

Writing the tests

For our first test, we'll use the MySQL command-line client to connect to the database we've configured and verify that we can log in using the username and password that we specified earlier. Because we're not applying the new roles and profiles to any machines, this test will fail when we run it. First, install the MYSQL client on the CI server. We'll use the following command to verify the connection to the database:

```
# yum install -y mariadb
```

Verify that the command was installed with the `which` command:

```
# which mysql
```

You should see `/bin/mysql` in the output.

Although we could write the test directly in the configuration for the build in Jenkins, it's a best practice to include tests with the source code. Create a directory named `test` at the top level of the Git repository to hold the test. Use the same checked-out version of the repository that we were using before with the same unprivileged user account:

```
$ cd ~/openstack/
$ mkdir test
```

Change into the `test` directory and create a shell script named `test.sh`, which attempts to connect to MySQL on the database node. The following script will suffice for now:

```
#!/bin/sh

/bin/mysql -h db.example.com -uroot -psecret -e "show databases;"
```

It should return the following output:

```
Can't connect to MySQL server.
```

Add the `test` directory to your commit and then commit and push your changes:

```
$ cd ../
$ git add test
$ git commit -m "adding first test case"
$ git push
```

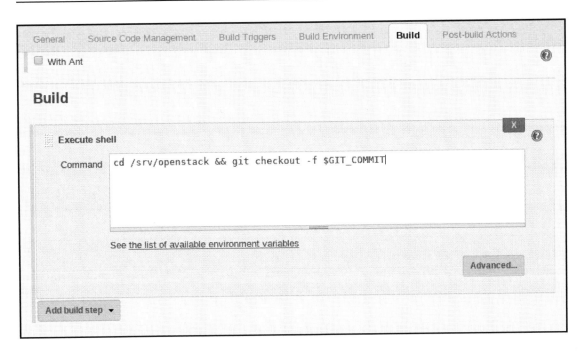

Once the code has been pushed, configure Jenkins to run the test. In the Jenkins UI, select the OpenStack project and click on **Configure** in the left-hand navigation. Under **Build**, click on **Add a build step** and select **Execute shell**. Enter the shell command, as shown in the following screenshot:

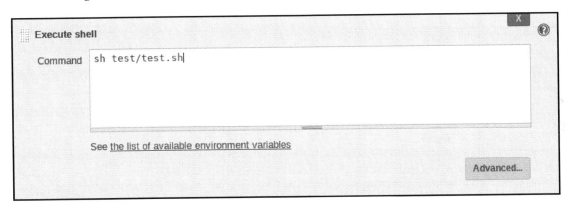

Save the configuration and select **Build Now** from the left-hand navigation. This build should fail.

Selecting **Console Output** should show the same error that we received when we ran the command on the command line. Now, let's set about configuring the database server to apply our profile and class so that the test will pass.

Assigning the first role to a system

To pull it all together, we'll start with a unconfigured system, install and configure the Puppet agent, and have it pull down the configuration that we've defined. Let's start by assigning the role to the system on the Puppet master.

As the root user on the CI server, create a `site.pp` file in `/etc/puppet/manifests`, which maps the unconfigured host to the role. For example, if my database host is named `db.example.com`, the following stanza will work:

```
node "db.example.com"
  include role::database
}
```

On the host itself, install the RDO repository and the Puppet agent with the following commands:

```
# yum install -y https://rdoproject.org/repos/rdo-release.rpm
# yum install -y puppet
```

Configure the system to use our CI server as its Puppet master. For example, if our CI server is `jenkins.example.com`, enter:

```
# puppet config set server 'jenkins.example.com' --section agent
```

Finally, do an initial Puppet run to set up the certificates:

```
# puppet agent -t
```

This should show the error `no certificate found` and `waitforcert` is disabled. Log in to the CI server as root and approve the certificate with the following command:

```
# puppet cert sign db.example.com
```

You will receive a notice that the certificate has been signed and the request has been removed.

Back on the database server, perform another Puppet run to pull the configuration:

```
# puppet agent -t
```

This will generate a lot of output as the system downloads all the Puppet modules from the master. You should see the system download, install, and configure MySQL databases for OpenStack. Finally, run a build from Jenkins again to see it succeed.

Installing Keystone

Let's iterate on the current environment, adding another profile and role. Now that we have a database available, install the first OpenStack service, Keystone. First, write a unit test. Our test will ensure that we can get a token from Keystone using the admin username and password that we specified in the Packstack answer file. This can be done with the `curl` command. Create a file named `test_keystone.sh` under the test directory in our Git repository:

```
$ cd ~/openstack/test/
$ vi test_keystone.sh
```

Use the following content as an example, substituting your password for the password of the demo user (secret) and the hostname for your first controller for controller01:

```
curl -i \
  -H "Content-Type: application/json" \
  -d '
  { "auth": {
    "tenantId": "demo",
    "passwordCredentials": {
      "userId": "demo",
      "password": "secret"
    }
  }
}' \
http://controller01:5000/v2/auth/tokens ; echo
```

Now run the script. It should fail with a `Connection refused` error.

To make the test pass, follow a process similar to the one we used to create the database profile. Create a file named `puppet/modules/openstack-profile/manifests/keystone.pp` in the OpenStack repository with the following contents:

```
class profile::keystone {
  include '::packstack::apache'
  include '::packstack::keystone'
}
```

Commit and push these files into the repository:

```
$ git add puppet/modules/openstack-profile/manifests/keystone.pp
$ git add puppet/modules/openstack-role/manifests/controller.pp
$ git commit -m 'adding a controller role and keystone profile'
$ git push
```

Run the build from Jenkins again to push the files to the Puppet master. We haven't configured Jenkins to run the new test yet, so the build should succeed, even though the test would fail.

Once again, take an unassigned machine and assign it the role of controller based on the hostname. In this example, we'll assign the role to a machine named `controller01.example.com`. Edit `/etc/puppet/manifests/site.pp` on the CI server and add the following stanza:

```
node "controller01.example.com" {
  include role::controller
}
```

On the unconfigured host named `controller01.example.com`, install the Puppet agent and set the Puppet master:

```
# yum install -y https://rdoproject.org/repos/rdo-release.rpm
# yum install -y puppet
# puppet config set server 'jenkins.example.com' --section agent
# puppet agent -t
```

Once again, you'll need to approve the certificate on the Puppet master:

```
# puppet cert sign controller01.example.com
```

On the second Puppet run, Keystone will be installed and configured. Enable the Keystone test that we wrote as a part of the commit in Jenkins by adding a new build step.

Run the build and ensure that the test passes now that Keystone is up-and-running on the first controller.

Fully automating the pipeline

Until now, we've been manually running both the Jenkins builds and the Puppet runs. This has allowed us to ensure that we're running the tests after the Puppet runs have finished. There are a few different ways to remove these two manual steps in the pipeline.

For the Jenkins build, Jenkins can either be configured to poll the source code repository every so often, or Git can be configured to reach out to Jenkins and trigger a build when new code is pushed. Jenkins can be configured to build either when the code is pushed to any branch or only when the code is pushed to a particular branch. This can allow you to ignore work in feature branches and only perform runs on merges to a master, or it can allow you to ignore merges and only perform runs on feature branches. Tools such as Stash and Bamboo provide for even easier integration.

Managing Puppet runs is a little more complex. By default, Puppet will run every 30 minutes or so, pick up changes from the Puppet master, and apply them. Although this makes sense for large environments that want to spread out the runs for performance, it can be frustrating to wait a half an hour for your environment to pick up the changes you just pushed to Git. There are two possible solutions to this problem. First, you can run Puppet on the hosts as a part of the test process. Tools such as Ansible can make this relatively simple. Second, you can decrease the interval between runs for your development environments. This is controlled by the runinterval setting in the main section of /etc/puppet/puppet.conf.

Once you've fully automated the pipeline, you'll want to add some kind of delay between the time that you push the changes to the Puppet master and the time that you run the unit tests. This will allow hosts to pick up the changes and implement them. For example, if you set the runinterval setting to 5 minutes and you expect changes to be applied within 5 minutes, you might add a build step in the Jenkins job that sleeps for 10 minutes before executing unit tests.

Summary

In this chapter, we talked about how organizations are using modern software development techniques to improve the quality of their OpenStack deployments. We built a simple deployment pipeline using Puppet, Git, and Jenkins, and we used it to deploy and test two components of the OpenStack infrastructure. From here, additional components can be installed, configured, and tested in a controlled fashion.

This can seem like a lot of extra effort for folks who are used to running Packstack and getting an environment up quickly. In our experience, though, without the proper infrastructure for managing and testing changes, these deployment become unwieldy at scale. As a reminder, the three basic tenets that we're following are:

- Small, manageable changes, not large upgrade cycles
- Test-driven development
- Continuous deployments

Because most organizations will already have some experience and tooling around these principles in software development, deployment pipelines vary greatly from organization to organization. A great example infrastructure to look at is the one that the OpenStack Foundation itself uses to test changes. More information on that pipeline is available at http://docs.openstack.org/infra/.

Further reading

Please refer to the following links for further reading:

- **OpenStack Puppet Guide**: http://docs.openstack.org/developer/puppet-openstack-guide/
- **OpenStack Ansible Project**: https://wiki.openstack.org/wiki/OpenStackAnsible
- **OpenStack Chef Project**: https://wiki.openstack.org/wiki/Chef
- **Designing Puppet - Roles and Profiles, Craig Dunn**: http://www.craigdunn.org/2012/05/239/
- **OpenStack Developer and Community Infrastructure Documentation**: http://docs.openstack.org/infra/

5
Building to Operate

A lot of OpenStack administrators are familiar with more established virtualization platforms. They're familiar with preinstalled operations tools that will allow an administrator to simply point, click, and configure a fully robust infrastructure, monitoring the solution in minutes. Unfortunately, OpenStack is not quite that simple. This doesn't mean it's inferior, quite the contrary; it's very flexible, and allows administrators to choose their own tools and configure them in a way that best suits the needs of the company or organization.

In this chapter, we will discuss day-2 operations, or in other words, what happens after the OpenStack cloud has been built, tested, and is operationally ready. It is at this point that the cloud is ready to onboard production users and workloads.

This chapter sets out to achieve the following:

- A critical insight into what is really important to monitor in an OpenStack cloud.
- A set of best practices to implement in a monitoring system. We will provide some example specifications to get you started and allow you to adjust them to meet your enterprise operation needs.
- Recommendations based on real-life examples of how to do effective capacity planning in an elastic cloud environment such as OpenStack.
- A broad understanding of some of the tools used in OpenStack operations, both open source and commercial.
- Transfer knowledge about future OpenStack operations in regards to artificial intelligence, machine learning, and in multi-cloud environments.

Logging, monitoring, and alerting

One of the most important aspects of operating an OpenStack cloud is **logging, monitoring, and alerting** (**LMA**). Since OpenStack isn't your legacy bare-metal-based infrastructure platform, it requires a different approach. The traditional LMA methods tend to fall short when considering the scale and elasticity of an OpenStack environment. Additionally, the old binary methods of alerting this service is down, the resource is at 95%, or even *filesystem full* messages do not deliver the depth of operational information really required to know the health of an OpenStack cloud. Since a cloud is an amalgamation of resources that are shared across a platform, it is the different services that clouds provide for network, storage, and compute that determines health versus the individual health of the underlying hardware components. In a properly configured HA architecture, OpenStack can withstand multiple underlying failures of infrastructure and only experience a decrease in capacity versus a total outage.

There are many different tools to actually monitor log events and create alerts from the underlying systems running the OpenStack infrastructure. However, in this chapter, we will focus more on the architectural principles that will help you choose your logging, monitoring, and alerting tools.

No matter what is used to do the logging, monitoring, and alerting, from an architectural standpoint, the solution should:

- Provide real-time, or near real-time introspection and alerting of events in the OpenStack infrastructure control layer
- Support some sort of discovery and configuration management
- Be scalable to support production enterprise clouds
- Have the ability to self-monitor and be configurable as highly available

Logging

An essential source of operational data for an OpenStack cloud is log data. Not only are the logs of host operating systems available, but each OpenStack project running as a part of the control plane has a separate log.

While the logs, by default, are sent to syslog and some of their own logs, it's recommended that all logs be sent to syslog under the same syslog log level as a starting point and modified if needed. This recommendation provides the greatest flexibility moving forward.

The following is an example of a successful operation in an OpenStack log entry from `nova-api.log`:

```
2017-07-08 07:36:45.613 3474 INFO nova.osapi_compute.wsgi.server [req-
b5ff3321-19cc-4ce8-af9c-0ed59ae21ac7 f32900acc09d4898b091b2caa4900112
6f0117ddd81b4dc78a8f4ce4dd5b04f5 - - -] 10.0.3.15 "GET
/v2/6f0117ddd81b4dc78a8f4ce4dd5b04f5/flavors/1 HTTP/1.1" status: 200 len:
613 time: 0.1168451
```

For security and analysis, all logs should be sent to a remote centralized syslog server. Ideally, this server will be where the log introspection, analytics, and cataloging will be done, and it should be hosted on a server with appropriate CPU and memory to support these workloads. Log introspection would be done on the content of the log entries as these logs can contain some, or all of the following (the example is based on the preceding log):

- Severity levels (INFO)
- The server that sent the log (`10.0.3.15`)
- The service that sent the log (`nova.osapi_compute.wsgi.server`)
- Metadata such as `tenant_id` and `request_id`
  (`6f0117ddd81b4dc78a8f4ce4dd5b04f5` and `req-b5ff3321-19cc-4ce8-af9c-0ed59ae21ac7`)

Request IDs are an integral part of troubleshooting OpenStack issues. They are generated each time a request is made of an OpenStack service. There are two different types of request IDs, global request IDs, and local request IDs. The main difference is that local request IDs are created by the individual services such as Nova, Glance, Cinder, and so on, and are only used within the service they were generated from. Global request IDs are passed from service to service to track the end-to-end status across the complete requested operation. This allows operators to use the request ID of a certain operation as a search key in common log analysis tools and can quickly determine the point of failure in an operation.

- Error codes from the service, and even performance data such as HTTP response times (involving limited usability for asynchronous connections due to the segmented nature of create requests and API interactions)

Here is what an error would look like:

```
nova-scheduler.log:2017-07-08 07:26:48.687 1159 ERROR
oslo.messaging._drivers.impl_rabbit [req-
c419cec6-9847-4692-8c61-733524097546 - - -
--] AMQP server on 10.0.3.15:5672 is unreachable: [Errno 111] ECONNREFUSED.
Trying again in 4 seconds
```

As we can see here, this is a structured log file that can be parsed by many different tools to extract the severity, service, timestamp, and other relevant metadata. Furthermore, this data could be parsed and searched with open source analysis tools such as **ElasticSearch, Logstash, and Kibana (ELK)** or **Splunk**. Basic information about ELK can be found at: https://www.elastic.co/webinars/introduction-elk-stack. This page also includes a webinar to get you started.

This concept of using a log processing platform, search platform, graphic dashboard, and an alerting platform is also being used as the OpenStack infrastructure monitoring solution at many large commercial and research production clouds. For example, CERN and GoDaddy are both using ELK to provide visibility into their OpenStack clouds. CERN's dashboard can be found here: http://openstack-in-production.blogspot.com/2013/10/log-handling-and-dashboards-in-cern.html.

However, not all solutions are ELK based; Mirantis, for example, is distributing a product it calls StackLight, which uses different log processing and formatting tools. It adds Grafana to the visual dashboard suite in addition to Kibana. You can refer to the example of Mirantis Cloud Platform's Devops Portal at: https://www.mirantis.com/software/mcp/stacklight/.

The most interesting log analysis, machine learning and AIOps solution for OpenStack is called **Loom** and is distributed by Loom Systems. It combines all of the log analysis above with machine learning and AI to reduce median time to recovery and does machine learning based correlation that shows administrators total root cause analysis across the complete enterprise. We will discuss this software a little further down in this chapter.

Monitoring

Many organizations struggle in the period between deployment and onboarding of applications. Most of this struggle is due to a lack of understanding of how OpenStack cloud operations differ from a typical legacy platform. Many times, this is the hardest barrier to overcome since it requires some fundamental cultural shifts in the way engineering, operations, and developers interact with infrastructure, applications, and platforms.

While some of the practices we will cover in this section may transpose over to workload monitoring, this chapter is about the operational monitoring of OpenStack infrastructure, not workloads running on OpenStack. Unlike OpenStack infrastructure, workloads running on the OpenStack cloud can be monitored by legacy platforms in many cases. There are many tools, both open source and commercial, that are purpose built to monitor workloads running on OpenStack clouds, but due to the broad availability of solutions in this sector, we will not be covering that topic in this chapter. We will instead concentrate on infrastructure monitoring.

What to monitor

In general, there are many categories of processes that support management by OpenStack. They are as follows:

- Stateless services and OpenStack API endpoints such as `nova-api`, `glance-api`, and `keystone-api`, that receive user inputs.
- OpenStack service workers connected to the message bus such as `nova-scheduler` and the placement API, that receives and processes user requests from other API-driven processes such as those listed earlier.
- Additional programs that are part of OpenStack and are not part of the actual codebase, but are more like enablers to the actual API layer, which provides services such as databases, replication, virtualization, and more. Some of these components are MySQL, RabbitMQ, Memcached, HAProxy, Corosync, and Pacemaker. Some of these elements are not in our Packstack environment since it is not a highly available environment; however, most production deployments by other distributions (Canonical, Red Hat, IBM, Suse, and so on) have these or other similar tools to provide similar functions. We will briefly mention these tools as they relate to operations and monitoring later in the chapter.
- The host operating system. In your installation, you may have installed RHEL or CentOS but OpenStack will run on most Linux distributions, including Ubuntu. Regardless of Linux distribution, the servers need a standard operating system, hardware, and capacity monitoring in order to ensure that the base of our install, the node itself, is operating properly. This monitoring can be an installed agent, agentless, IPMI, SSH, or any other interfaces depending on the monitoring platform.

- Network hardware, routers, switches, firewalls, and so on will all need to be monitored; however, these are typically external to the OpenStack infrastructure and are not part of our Packstack install. If you are integrating an SDN solution into OpenStack, it will typically plug into Neutron and run from existing or dedicated network nodes. These will also need to be monitored as infrastructure nodes as well as specialized third-party software nodes that may contain additional databases or messaging servers, depending on the solution.
- External storage should be monitored by the respective business unit that is providing the storage to the cloud. While there are a number of options to connect storage to OpenStack nodes through fiber channel, iSCSI, or NAS, monitoring this storage is beyond the scope of this book. One exception to this recommendation is made by distributed storage platforms, such as Ceph, that are often bundled with some OpenStack distributions. Ceph should be monitored with the command line or tools such as Calamari (Red Hat Storage Console/Tendri), Intel VSM, InkScope, ceph-dash, or OpenAttic.

Monitoring practices

The following are some distinct monitoring practices that are aimed at addressing different parts of a total holistic monitoring approach. These practices can be classified into three categories—availability, performance, and usage. Together, these practices make up a solid foundation for any monitoring strategy. While there may be additional components depending on industry and corporate requirements, the majority of operational use cases should fit into the cases as follows:

Monitoring availability

Availability monitoring, at its core, is really any monitoring activity that supports the inspection of resources for OpenStack compute, storage, and networking, as well as the endpoints that support user interaction with those resources (OpenStack service APIs). Availability can be defined as simply available versus not available or as granular as specific **Service-Level Agreements (SLAs)**.

In order to measure availability, there are key metrics that can be used as indicators. They provide a status in regard to the availability of a resource, and they can also provide empirical data on how many resources are currently available. This availability check can be accomplished by running synthetic or real tests against the environment that mimic the behavior of real users. One caveat of synthetic testing is to limit the amount and frequency of the testing to prevent causing load on the control plane. Some examples of synthetic tests include:

- Creating/deleting/updating users
- Creating/deleting/updating volumes
- Creating/deleting/updating VMs
- Keystone operations involving token creation and verification
- If using ironic, basic operations with bare-metal provisioning and discovery

Monitoring performance

Monitoring performance typically measures the responsiveness of a process, connection, or workflow. In cloud computing, it is typically used to define how long it takes to complete certain workflows. Some of these workflows are—creating instances, volumes, networks, or other OpenStack resources. The key metrics from the performance can usually be extracted from OpenStack service logs and the timestamps that they contain. Since provisioning an instance is a multi-project workflow, performance impacts can be traced end to end using start and finish times per project per request, as well as between project handoffs. Other methods of measuring performance may use the output from OpenStack commands using native time measurement tools, as well as by modifying the OpenStack code to add instrumentation.

Monitoring resource usage

In this section, we will only partially use resource usage monitoring. In a later section, we will cover it in more depth as it relates to capacity planning. However, the purpose of resource usage monitoring is that an operator can, at will, retrieve the amount of resources being used by not only one user, but also a tenant, or the entire cloud through the OpenStack APIs. This monitoring does not have to be performed in real time. In most instances, resource monitoring is an activity which is done with data that has been collected over a specific period of time. Later in this chapter, we will cover the Ceilometer project, which is the metering project for OpenStack.

Alerting

The alerting process is one of the most important steps in any operational model. Alerting is the process by which the monitoring platform alerts the operator about a situation that is outside the set thresholds. These alerts can be delivered in a multitude of ways from ticketing platforms such as Remedy, email, SMS, IRC, or even integrations with communication platforms such as Slack (`https://slack.com/`), HipChat, or PagerDuty. These alerts should contain the basic information regarding the event that triggered them. This could be any key value that has either gone from a good state to a non-good state or a key value that has breached a SLA level. In all cases, these alerts are driven by a change in state and may not be a direct indication of a problem, but may be an indication of a future issue.

Therefore, alerts should:

- Display which OpenStack service is affected
- Contain a general description of the change in state that caused the alert if implemented, and have a severity level defined by the operational staff
- Have the ability to be marked as a false positive or be disabled during events such as maintenance
- Have the ability to chain alerts together in a logical fashion to trigger additional actions and provide rudimentary correlation
- Provide the ability to refer to time-series statistics such as median, percentile, and standard deviation
- Provide an instant view of services that are in a good, warning, or failed state
- Not be so frequent as to cause alert fatigue and ultimately result in auto closure

Most warnings and errors seen in a correctly configured OpenStack environment are not critical in nature and do not indicate a complete outage. Most errors in OpenStack environments are usually due to spurious failed instance provisions or other similar non-outage warnings. Remember, even if the OpenStack control plane has a complete failure, the workloads will continue to run (in most cases). Therefore, having a monitoring solution that can determine the proper alerting level for a warning or error is critical. This resolves issues of overalerting operations personnel and causing them undue fatigue or requiring them to troubleshoot minor warnings. With overalerting, the warnings may simply be an indication of something minor and should be watched as a trend indicator instead of a call to action. A simple alert requirement would consist of policies similar to the following:

- Critical errors, resulting in failure states, should always be reported in an alert and require immediate action.

- Other problems in OpenStack HA environments, for example, one failed service on one controller in an environment with three controllers, should not be marked as critical, but marked as a warning or deferred state to indicate a degradation of high availability.
- Warnings should be evaluated for frequency and consistency. If they are the result of deprecated command switches or minor configuration issues, they may be safely ignored once it is determined that they will not be remediated.

A great way to test the capacity of an OpenStack cloud before it is placed into production is to run a load generator against a staging cloud that is built to mirror the production environment. One open source project, named Rally (`http://rally.readthedocs.io/en/latest/index.html`), is a great tool to identify functional failures and performance bottlenecks in your environment. The following diagram describes the basic functions of the tool. It uses another tool named **Tempest** to run standard load tests against OpenStack. It has a web interface to specify limits and examine results in graphical reports:

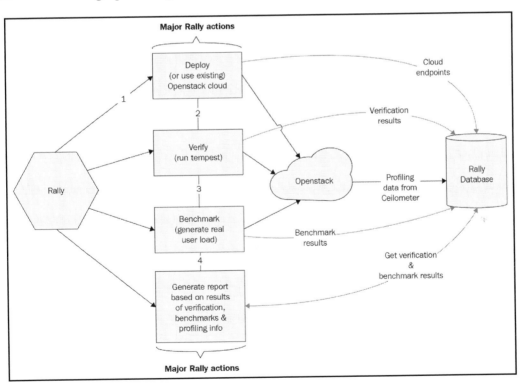

Rally actions

Active monitoring

There are quite a few activities to monitor in OpenStack. In general, there are three major areas to monitor:

- OpenStack services (required for orchestration and provisioning)
- Processes (the actual running processes of OpenStack components)
- HA control cluster (the components providing HA capability to the cloud)

Services

Checking services is all about availability. If a service is down, cloud users will be faced with errors that prevent them from using the APIs and, furthermore, interacting with the cloud. These service checks should be performed regularly using simulated transactions generated from the monitoring platform. We call these simulated because they do not require all the specific customizations of the image and post-deployment configuration that may be needed for real workloads. While using real workloads is possible, it is less desirable due to the additional overhead needed to run actual transactions on a regular basis, in addition to the real deployment load. Synthetic transactions should be launched from a dedicated user in their own project with strict quotas. This way, the transactions can be tracked using tenant and user IDs that are separate from real traffic.

These checks should be launched against the VIP addresses for endpoints (if configured in an HA configuration) and only report two possible options—completed or failed. This way, the tests can be contained to simple operations. Complex simulations will involve other endpoints and may provide false positives. For example, if the Nova API endpoint were to be tested, a good test would be to check the flavors associated with the monitoring tenant. An example call to the API to the Nova project would be as follows:

```
GET /v2.1/{tenant_id}/flavors
```

Additional API specifications can be found at: http://developer.openstack.org/.

In order to make this API call through a monitoring platform such as Nagios, the platform could be configured to use the nova CLI client for the Nova project from a plugin script, or a set of plugin scripts, which would call the API through Python or another scripted language. These plugin scripts, many of which are available for free at `http://www.nagios.com`, can be leveraged to check the API endpoint status using simulated actions. For example, some OpenStack infrastructure plugins have been contributed to the Nagios directory such as the one called `check_nova_api` from *Rakesh Patnaik* at `https://github.com/rakesh-patnaik/nagios-openstack-monitoring`, which checks the API service for Nova using Python and a direct call to the Nova API endpoint. The `nagios-openstack-monitoring` plugins not only have the capabilities to monitor the API endpoints but the plugin also contains scripts to check the processes.

Processes

Many individual processes support the operation of OpenStack. Many of these processes run on the controller nodes and need to be running in order to provide API availability (the `nova-api` process) as well as processes that coordinate functionality to other parts of the control stack (mariaDB and RabbitMQ). These processes can be checked locally, through remote SSH agents driven by shell scripts, or through automation enabled by software such as Ansible, Chef, and Puppet. Additionally, as aforementioned, there are plugins for monitoring platforms, such as Nagios, ZenOs, and Zabbix, that also include these process checks.

HA control cluster

Many different distributions use HAProxy to enable active/active availability across multiple OpenStack control servers (a minimum of three). This HAProxy service acts as a reverse proxy and simple load balancer configured to listen to VIP addresses in front of the OpenStack endpoint addresses. It is a common practice to have HAProxy running on each one of the controller nodes in an HA cluster. Since the HAProxy service is tied to the VIP addresses configured for the OpenStack API services, if these services fail under HAProxy, then HAProxy itself will fail over to another controller node for the service. However, HAProxy does not monitor or fail over the processes, nor does it move the VIP addresses to other cluster members. Therefore, an additional tool such as pacemaker or keepalived should be used to satisfy this requirement.

The following diagram shows a logical diagram of one way to configure HA controllers:

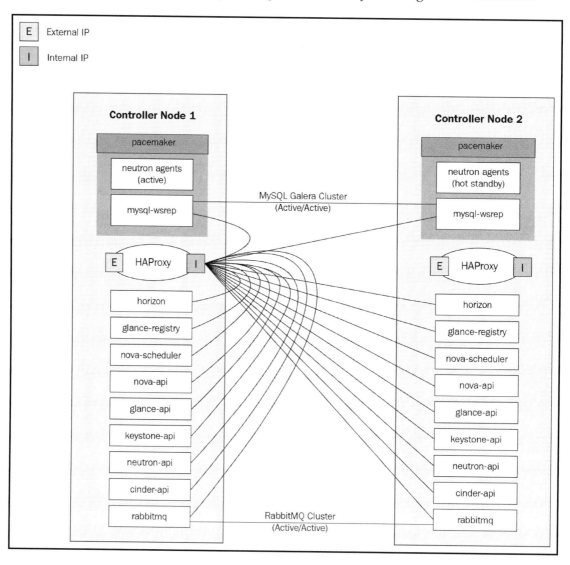

Mirantis OpenStack controller HA architecture - Mirantis

More information on this topic can be found at: `http://docs.openstack.org/ha-guide/controller-ha-haproxy.html`. Alternatively, there is also the ability to use other external software or hardware load balancers instead of HAProxy.

Given this architecture for OpenStack Control Plane HA, and the monitoring of processes on each of the HA control nodes, it is possible that in a three-node cluster, two of the three controllers' processes for a single project can be completely down and OpenStack will still be completely functional. This is why, as in service monitoring, process states and overall health alerts must be customized very carefully. Simply because one controller's individual process (for example, `nova-api`) fails and the HA infrastructure is still operational, does not mean that the monitoring solution should display a critical alert that the OpenStack cloud has failed.

A dashboard example

SUSE OpenStack Cloud Monitoring
(`https://www.suse.com/documentation/suse-openstack-cloud-7/singlehtml/monitor-osoperator/monitor-osoperator.html`) provides a set of visualizations that can be configured to create a monitoring overview of your services. It provides a simple, clean interface for checking running services and alerting on log irregularities. This tool leverages another open source OpenStack project called Monasca at the heart of its monitoring-as-a-service offering.

Dynatrace (`https://www.dynatrace.com`) has also developed a plugin to its popular Application Performance Management solution to have some introspection into its OpenStack environments by showing resource utilization and the availability of OpenStack services by using log data and other tools, as shown at: `https://dt-cdn.net/wp-content/uploads/2017/07/openstack-dashboard1.png`.

There are many other third-party tools that have their own opinionated logging, monitoring, and alerting solutions. However, despite their differences in choices of open source and closed source software, they all pretty much have similar architectures and provide similar functionality to our previous examples. At the heart of their solutions, they are all based on the log analysis fundamentals discussed earlier in this chapter.

The future of OpenStack troubleshooting and Artificial Intelligence-driven operations

As systems and workloads become increasingly abstracted, the velocity, frequency, and variety of data continues to multiply at exponential rates. At one time, many years ago, it was sufficient for administrators to simply log into servers that were unresponsive and comb through a handful of log files in order to determine **root cause analysis** (RCA).

Today, for example, in OpenStack, there are more than 15 different log files created by OpenStack control plane servers, as well as multiple unique logs in each of the compute servers. All of these logs, combined with logs from the operating systems, routers, switches, load balancers, WAN compressors equals a mountain of data to search in order to find a true incident RCA. The voracity, velocity and volume of data to search through manually decreases an administrator's ability to find RCA and solve issues. This, plus the number of new servers added to enterprises daily are contributing to a climbing **Mean Time To Recovery** (MTTR). Today, 3 hours is the average time it takes IT professionals to repair a single problem. That is simply unacceptable when we want our latest purchases delivered to our house via drone in 30 minutes.

One of the recent technological use cases around cloud computing has been **machine learning** (ML) and **Artificial Intelligence** (AI). The ability to harness capacity on demand and configure large clusters of systems to power massive parallel processing of data is quickly becoming a reality. Some companies are taking this concept of AI one step further and using operational data to enable what is being called **Artificial Intelligence Operations** (AIOps). These platforms are using correlation and resolution data to help administrators arrive at an RCA quicker by continually scanning log files in real time. As logs stream into the platform they need to recognize where there may be a problem by correlating across multiple log files, correlating the log sections by applying complex rules across multiple devices, and even multiple environments.

One such company, Loom Systems (https://www.loomsystems.com/), has created **Loom Cloud Intelligence** (LUCI), which provides a solution to the log sprawl problem by applying an AI to monitor all platforms and systems in a single plane of glass. LUCI, shown in the screenshot below, has the ability to see and correlate all IT sources in real time and push alerts via legacy alerting or using ChatOps. LUCI also allows administrators to drill down on alerts and correlated issues and creates stories of incidents based on empirical data retrieved from numerous log files.

LUCI also suggests possible RCA and remediations based on AI-driven problem determination. Loom Systems supports many different platforms including OpenStack, VMware, AWS, Microsoft Azure, and Google Cloud. Loom has a SaaS solution as well as an on-premise solution for those who cannot send log data offsite:

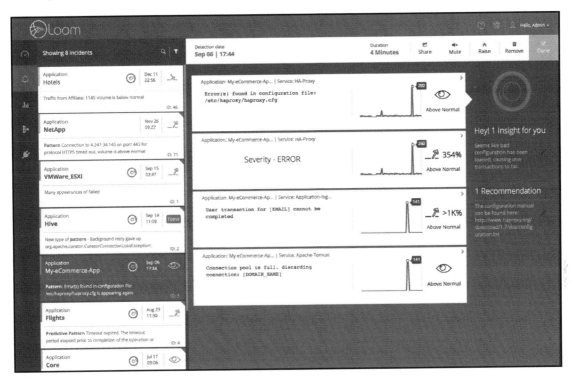

LUCI from Loom Systems

AIOps tools such as LUCI are becoming a necessity in enterprises based on the amounts of systems, both ephemeral and persistent, that are being used as a holistic solution to application development. With the onslaught of containers, serverless computing, and multi-cloud, simple log analysis and monitoring platforms will need to evolve into self-driven learning platforms in order to keep up with the pace of innovation. The next step is self-remediation and capacity scaling based on live streaming behavioral data, sector trending, customer behaviors, and so on.

Capacity planning

As one of the four major ITIL processes that fall under financial management for IT, capacity planning is clearly an important part of any cloud strategy. However, not all cloud strategies are the same. It is very important to differentiate workloads in enterprise virtualization and in an OpenStack elastic cloud. With virtualization, each workload, and in many cases each server, is important. If an individual virtualization server becomes overused or is somehow degraded, that particular server is investigated, scaled, and/or repaired. One common analogy is to compare virtualized VMs and servers to *pets*. In the pure OpenStack cloud world, there is no such construct for these individual instances (pets) except when virtualized workloads are moved into the elastic cloud and thus bring IT-as-a-service workloads into a true cloud. OpenStack was constructed around the premise that workloads are ephemeral, failure is expected, and growth should be scaled horizontally, not vertically. If a workload fails, another will simply be started in its place. *Livestock* has been the analogy used to explain this idea of ephemeral instances and workloads. In this analogy, livestock are simply a resource; if they die, or are irreparably injured, they are simply destroyed and replaced. In OpenStack, this idea even extends to the underlying hardware. In many companies, compute servers are simply white label hardware compute server resources that are to be used on-demand. If they fail, other online and equally ubiquitous resources take their place (either in a scripted disaster recovery fashion or by having adequate excess capacity). Furthermore, if the compute servers become slow due to high loads, more ubiquitous resources (compute servers) are added to increase capacity. This is an important concept to grasp when speaking about elastic capacity. Under this definition of compute, servers are generically uniform, disposable, and scalable resources, and when the available capacity changes, growth is not linear but based on demand. However, demand can change with development cycles, development methodologies, time of the year, and production cycles.

This variability of demand is typically linear and possibly exponential based on cloud adoption. However, proper methodologies are required when constructing an OpenStack environment to help develop the most accurate capacity planning and provide a foundation to create strategic and tactical decisions later. This differs quite a bit from virtualization capacity planning, which tends to be more linear since the workloads are more persistent and are not recycled very frequently.

Planning your city

Very similar to civil planning and architecture, the OpenStack cloud is a city of tenants that require resources to exist. However, with limited resources, tenants cannot be left to self-manage; the risk of resource exhaustion is too great. This would be analogous to the residents of an apartment building having unlimited power, water, gas, cable, and space without metering or charging for anything. Many residents would probably operate under the assumption that the resources were unlimited and they could oversize and oversubscribe to everything without consequence. Therefore, it is up to operations, both in civil engineering and OpenStack clouds, to do capacity management and risk mitigation for the end user. This means finding a way to track, analyze, and gather payment (or at least show costs) from end users or their tenant cost center. This includes creating packages of structured resources that are predetermined, which users can select from, as well as creating and maintaining a quota system.

Capacity risk mitigation and planning are done by performing three distinct actions:

- Track usage
- Analyze growth
- Chargeback/showback

Tracking usage and analyzing growth

In order to track usage of any resource, we first need to standardize the units we plan to count. In cloud computing, extreme granularity is possible using the data that exists in OpenStack databases, as well as using the metering project, Ceilometer. While there are many different meters that can be tracked, let's start by tracking the number of individual vCPUs used over time, amounts of memory over time, and disk usage down to the minute. However, letting users put together their own combinations of these three data points can result in tens of thousands of combinations. Therefore, in the OpenStack cloud, we use flavors to limit user choices. Flavors are virtual hardware templates that are logical groupings of compute, storage, and even network elements.

This simplifies the chargeback/showback equation by logically grouping resources into manageable offerings. In our examples, we will only be considering vCPU and memory; however, the same principles can be applied to persistent and ephemeral storage as well as network resource allocation.

Continuing with our analogy of civil engineering, we can think of a flavor as an extended family looking to occupy an apartment building with a set of space requirements. In this example, one constraint we will have is that the 65,536 sq/ft building can only have a maximum of 16 rooms and by code, can only hold 64 people. However, since this is a new apartment building, the room sizes have not been determined and the property manager will build the rooms to match the family's requirements. The property manager decides to let the first three applicants pick sizes for their rooms and he will bill them for whatever specifications the families need.

Let's start with each family's requests, each with exact and unique requirements:

- 3-person family requiring 1,024 sq/ft
- 7-person family requiring 8,096 sq/ft
- 29-person family requiring 30,720 sq/ft

In the following diagram, we can see what a sample 65,536 sq/ft house would look like using these unique and arbitrary room sizes:

We now have a total of 49 people and their belongings occupying the building with a capacity of 64. That leaves room for 15 more people spread across a lot of wasted space (resources) of all types and configurations since no more of the existing family groupings listed fit nicely into equal rooms in the existing space. The property manager only has two choices. He can create additional odd-sized apartments to fit 15 more people of different families and hope that families of that size apply, or buy a new house and continue to use the existing odd sizes while abandoning the wasted space in the property. This is what happens in an OpenStack cloud when flavor standardization does not take place.

Consider a compute node as a cargo van and flavors as boxes. With standard size boxes come ease of packing and high efficiency. Consider the boxes as vCPUs; for now, we will consider that the boxes are all square with the following measurements:

- 1 ft wide box
- 2 ft wide box
- 4 ft wide box

Most of the boxes people ship on this route are of the 2 ft flavor, but two other types of boxes are also available (1 ft and 4 ft). However, the Department of Transportation only allows 64 ft of boxes per truck. However, this time, we created spaces that were stackable. We can now see what happens when we have structured groupings of boxes that are exponents of one another:

As you can see, we now have 64 ft of boxes in the cargo van; since we've controlled our box (flavor) sizings and made them standard, we make it easy for the cargo loader (or in OpenStack's case, resource management programs such as nova-scheduler/cinder-scheduler) to do the placement. We are no longer wasting a lot of resources or space. As a result, efficiency is increased. Since efficiency is high, capacity planning becomes much easier and more predictable.

Of course, the preceding example used only one resource for sizing, vCPU. The sizing becomes more difficult when we add RAM, and possibly storage sizing, with each OpenStack flavor. We can think of flavors as nesting tables. In order to get the most efficiency, the tables have to be a fraction of the largest size. Another way to think of this is packing a box with the smaller boxes. If you can fit many combinations of the smaller boxes in the larger box, with no wasted space, you have a winning flavor combination. OpenStack flavor resources should follow these same recommendations:

- Determine the most common flavor in use in your organization today
- Double (t x 2) the most used flavor and it will be your largest offering (double any resources that need to fit the nesting method for capacity planning)
- Halve (t x 0.5) the most used flavor and it will be your smallest offering
- If you have additional flavors that are larger or smaller, increase or decrease by this same amount

Flavor sizing and compute server hardware selection

Since typical workloads call for multiples of 2 in vCPU and RAM (1,024 MB), this works out particularly well when the compute hardware is sized based on the most common flavor of an organization. Unfortunately, many organizations buy hardware first, then create OpenStack clouds; others reuse hardware from existing environments. By designing compute server hardware configurations around workloads, maximum efficiency can be gained.

For example, an average flavor in an organization could be a 2 vCPU with 4,096 MB of RAM. Doubling of this common flavor would result in a 4 vCPU flavor with 8,192 MB of RAM. The smallest flavor would then be calculated at half of the middle flavor (one-fourth of the largest flavor at 1 vCPU and 2,048 MB of RAM). Other flavors could be added above and below these flavors and named XL and Tiny, but for illustrative purposes, we will stick with only 3.

In order to determine compute capacity, we use the desired VM density that is desired; for this discussion, we will set the estimate at 40 VMs per compute server and multiply the density by the organization's most common flavor:

40 x 2 vCPU = 80 vCPU (assuming non-hyperthreaded CPU, multiply this number by 1.3 for hyperthreading)

40 x 4096 = 160 GB RAM (assuming a 1:1 ratio of RAM subscription)

As a rule of thumb, compute nodes require about 20% of the total vCPU and RAM for overhead and OS processes when fully loaded. These resources need to be included in the calculations for total resources needed:

*Required number of vCPUs with OS overhead: 80 * 1.20 (100% + 20%) = 96 vCPU*

*Required memory with OS overhead: 160 * 1.20 = 192 GB RAM*

Therefore, in order to have an accurately scaled starting point, we would need a compute server with the hardware to support 96 vCPUs. We will set the overcommit ratio at 8:1 for vCPUs, and therefore we would need to divide the number of required vCPUs by 8 to get the number of the CPU cores we need. Overcommit ratios may vary, so adjust your calculation to match, as shown here:

Total number of vCPUs needed / Overcommit = Cores

96 / 8 = 12 CPU cores

Therefore, based on this calculation, we need 12 CPU cores for about 40 instances of the average flavor of this cloud, named medium. Since most servers come as dual-core or quad-core models now, we would simply need a single dual core CPU with a 6-core processor. For this example, something like the Intel E5-2620v3 or E5-2643v3 would be sufficient for generalized workloads.

For memory, we simply need to ensure that each compute server has 192 GB of RAM, and since this is a 6-dual-core single CPU server with 12 DIMM banks, each bank would require 32 GB per processor bank. Therefore, as a visual representation, the following diagram is roughly what the logical memory allocation could look like:

 There are some spare resources remaining after the server has reached its 40-instance limit plus one. This memory could be used for an additional instance or left as a reserve for compute server OS spikes at a load.

In the preceding figure, we have a breakdown, as shown here:

Flavor size	Instances	vCPUs	Memory (GB)
Small	13	13	26
Medium	24	48	96
Large	4	16	32
Total	41	78	154
Reserved for OS		18 (~20%)	38 GB (~20%)

This shows an almost ideal configuration for our earlier flavor requirements, even though we didn't fill it with all medium-sized images. However, if more flavors had been added without adhering to the recommended preceding model, we would end up with gaps and wasted CPU and memory depending on the flavor diversity and number of instances of those flavors.

Using this flavor determinism as a best practice will allow operators to more accurately measure/monitor the following:

- Overall capacity
- Growth over time
- Utilization and overutilization
- Correct VM placement by Nova

Many companies have spent considerable time developing in-house strategies for collecting, managing, and analyzing data from their clouds to answer the topics discussed. However, in recent years, many different **Cloud Management Platforms** (**CMPs**) and purpose-built monetization and management software have emerged to simplify chargeback and showback. However, there have been scale challenges around OpenStack's telemetry project, Ceilometer. Advances in technology have been made; however, some capacity planning software is now configured to use the OpenStack APIs directly and does not even need the OpenStack telemetry service (Ceilometer).

Capacity in the cloud must be part of a more deterministic type of capacity planning methodology. Keeping the appropriate elasticity at all times is a tricky business and must be carefully monitored to achieve a balance between availability and depreciation of resources. Users tend to believe that cloud resources are infinite; sadly, however, they are not. All requests for resources, even paravirtualized ones, are simply mapped back to groups of physical devices that have limits.

Unfortunately, end users tend to not know or somehow forget this paradigm. As a result, at times, end users fall back into a hoarding behavior when they are not charged or tracked for resource consumption. Unfortunately, this behavior is most likely the by-product of years of legacy infrastructure processes taking months before developer teams were able to obtain additional infrastructure. With these limits and demands in mind, it is increasingly important for cloud administration or operations to take charge of capacity planning for all aspects of the OpenStack cloud. The easiest way to take charge of this behavior is through chargeback or showback. This allows OpenStack administrators to give users an account of what they are consuming on a regular basis. Additionally, if chargeback is enabled, it is a way for cloud groups or public providers to recoup the costs of maintaining an elastic environment.

In order to be able to show and charge users for resources, administrators need to follow the preceding capacity planning recommendations as well as providing cloud users with features such as periodic statements, the cost for resources before deploying, running costs, and payment or billing options. While most software that can perform this functionality is in the commercial realm, there are a few open source tools that can be leveraged to provide some features.

Some examples of leading capacity planning and charge back solutions are as follows:

Name	Company	Open/closed source	Supports	Website
CloudKitty	Objectif Libre	Open source	OpenStack	`https://wiki.openstack.org/wiki/CloudKitty`
HP	Cloud Optimizer 3.0	Closed source	OpenStack AWS Xen VMware Hyper-V	`https://software.microfocus.com/en-us/products/operations-bridge-suite/overview`
Red Hat	Cloudforms ManageIQ	Closed source Open source	OpenStack AWS Google	`https://access.redhat.com/documentation/en-us/red_hat_cloudforms/4.1/` `http://manageiq.org/`

Backups and recovery

Typically, backups and recovery aren't the first things traditional OpenStack operators think of. This is usually because of the ephemeral workloads traditionally run on OpenStack clouds, which really didn't persist long enough to be backed up. However, as OpenStack adoption has grown exponentially, we are seeing more and more production OpenStack deployments that include persistent workloads, especially in IT-as-a-Service clouds. As a result, a need has arisen to back up critical infrastructure data as well as persistent workloads running on the cloud.

Infrastructure backup architecture

While workloads running on an OpenStack cloud are the stars of the show, the infrastructure is the real hero. Keeping the APIs available and running 100% without interruption should be the end goal of any operator when it comes to availability. However, it's simply not reality. Even with proper life cycle management and change procedures, data corruption can happen. Since the heart of OpenStack is a structured database running on MariaDB, it only makes sense to run it in a highly available configuration. However, what happens if, during operation, errors are made and are replicated across all HA nodes? Failure. Now, without backup and recovery, not only are the APIs offline, and the workloads could still be online, but all the data about every instance and the network configuration for those instances are lost. This is a true disaster for any OpenStack cloud.

Backup strategies – what to back up

There is some critical data that must be backed up regularly in order to ensure proper recovery of OpenStack cloud. The frequency of these backups should align with your recovery time objective (the time to cloud restoration after a disaster in order to avoid unacceptable consequences to business continuity). There may also be recovery point objectives and SLAs within your organization that you may have to adhere to. While these are more common to disaster recovery regarding persistent workloads and not the infrastructure, there are always exceptions.

Critical items you should back up to be able to recover from a full or partial disaster are listed in the following table:

Data item	Project	Location	Instructions
MySQL DB	Openstack DB	Controller	Use mysqldump to export the contents of the database. Copy the data to a backup server.
Nova	Compute	Compute controller	Make copies of /etc/nova and copy to the backup server. Make copies of /var/lib/nova except /var/lib/nova/instances on compute nodes. Instance backups will be discussed later.
Glance	Image Repo	Controller	Copy the /etc/glance and /var/lib/glance directories, or rsync /var/lib/glance/images to another backup server.
Keystone	Identity	Controller	Back up /etc/keystone. Back up /var/lib/keystone if there is any data in it.
Cinder	Block Storage	Controller	Back up /etc/cinder. Back up /var/lib/cinder.
Swift	Object Storage	Controller	Back up /etc/swift; it contains the configuration files as well as the ring and ring builder files. Without these, your data is completely inaccessible. Copy these to every storage node before backing them up.

Once all of these files have been backed up and moved to a secure on-site or off-site disaster recovery server, in order to restore your OpenStack cloud you will basically need to stop all services on the existing cloud, copy all of the files back into place, recover the database from the export, and restart the cloud.

While this looks simple, it takes time. If this plan looks like it won't meet your RTO needs, there are ways to make OpenStack highly available and create an architecture that is both multi-cloud and multi-region while having the ability to fail over and recover to a completely different site during a disaster. These solutions involve replication of Cinder storage across WAN links, a custom migration middleware solution, and a network plan to bring up the disaster recovery cloud online with all of the access and configurations it needs to satisfy business requirements. This solution can be extended by replicating database metadata and having a global object store for Glance images; however, as you can imagine, this is quite a feat of architecture and engineering and beyond the scope of this book.

Workload backup architecture

As mentioned previously, workloads are the reason that a cloud even exists. In a perfect world, all applications would be cloud-native, fully distributed, and 12 factor apps. They wouldn't require backups because they would be regionally or globally distributed across multiple clouds and horizontally scaled to autoscale in the case of a disaster in one location. However, that is simply not the reality for many organizations. Many organizations have the need to run persistent workloads and traditional applications in production clouds. However, the legacy methods of backing up these applications, especially in bare metal environments, are drastically different. With most resources being virtualized and tenant networks isolated, traditional backup and restore architectures simply do not apply in OpenStack. Therefore, not only do organizations need a disaster recovery backup solution for workloads, but they also need operational backup solutions, sometimes known as **Backup-as-a-Service (BaaS)**.

Planning for disaster recovery

Since workloads that require backup on OpenStack consist mainly of persistent instances, we must back up all parts of the instance; not only the disk image(s) that holds all of the runtime and persistent data but also the metadata that is required to make the workload instance(s) able to be restored from backup. However, OpenStack lacks the ability to provide a policy-based, automated, comprehensive backup and recovery solution. While OpenStack provides a patchwork of tools and APIs to provide some sort of backup effort, even tools such as OpenStack's Cinder API, which provides support for taking full and incremental volume snapshots, are still disruptive and the workload has to be taken offline to take a snapshot or risk data corruption.

To illustrate this, we can look at the typical steps to do a simple backup on a basic workload:

1. Pause instances
2. Detach Cinder volumes (root volume and any additional non-root volumes)
3. Take an instance snapshot for each instance and store it in Glance for later retrieval
4. Use Cinder to back up all the aforementioned volumes and place them in Object Storage (Swift/Ceph)
5. Document these copies since OpenStack does not track them for you
6. Resume instances

These steps are very command intensive, take time, require custom scripts, and since there is a manual documentation step, could be error-prone. These steps may also not adhere to existing internal backup policies of the organization.

This manual type of backup operation is antiquated and feature limited. Any enterprise-level backup solution should be non-impacting, able to do incremental backups and be customized for each workload, and able to span multiple instances when workloads are also spread across instances. Additionally, tenants should be able to easily back up their own workloads and test them before committing them to storage and have the ability to restore and replay backups when they desire. Workload backup software should also be able to provide a disaster recovery component so that in the event of a catastrophe, backed-up and replicated resources are available at different geographic locations, in case any single location is compromised.

There are few open source and commercial options when considering workload backup solutions that use native snapshots from OpenStack. One open source option is called Raksha (https://wiki.openstack.org/wiki/Raksha), the OpenStack project version of what became TrilioVault (http://www.triliodata.com/about/), a commercial data protection, backup, and disaster recovery solution specifically designed for OpenStack. Trilio Data has taken the previously mentioned workload backup snapshot procedure and designed a flexible and scalable solution. Using TrilioVault, both full and incremental backups of snapshots can be stored on a wide range of storage including NFS, Swift, and other third-party arrays. Recovery is also GUI-driven and simplifies what would otherwise be driven by sets of homegrown scripts to launch backup and recovery actions. TrilioVault also provides additional features for data retention, protection, and data integrity.

Additionally, traditional file-based backup solutions can be run inside OpenStack and can be used as BaaS offerings. While we can't cover every BaaS option, the following table compares some common options from some software used by enterprise customers today. This BaaS model is typically used by cloud providers, both public and private, to offer backup services to clients. These are priced with a cost model based on capacity, bandwidth, the number of clients, and so on. Cloud backup services leverage the shared private cloud infrastructure, just like other cloud services, and are infrastructure-abstracted. BaaS can be leveraged by both tenants inside the cloud as well as external hosts that desire to back up into the cloud.

At this time, Trilio Data's TrilioVault (`www.trilio.io`) is the only native OpenStack backup solution. It provides tenant-level backup and recovery solutions for OpenStack clouds only. Trilio generates full and incremental point-in-time backups of tenant's application containers and the network, compute, security, and metadata configurations that are associated with it. It provides file level and whole recovery of client VMs and configurations. Other options include:

Features and common requirements	Trilio Data - TrilioVault	Cloudberry	Commvault Simpana	Community Amanda (open source)
File-based backup	Yes	Yes	Yes	Yes
Client-server architecture	Yes	Can be both	Yes	Yes
Data formats available	NFS/Swift/S3	Swift Object Storage	Native dump/SCSI	Native dump and/or GNU tar
Deduplication	Yes	Yes	Yes	No
DR to remote site	Yes	Yes	Yes	No
Encryption and compression	No	Yes	Yes	Yes
Incremental backups	Yes	No	Yes	Yes
LDAP integration	Yes	Workaround	Yes	Workaround
Licensing	Annual or Multiyear	Annual, Permanent	Annual	Free
OpenStack Native	Yes	No	No	No
Cinder/Nova Integration	Yes	No	No	No
Linux client	Yes	No	Yes	Yes
MS Exchange	N/A	Yes	Yes	Workaround

MS SharePoint	N/A	Workaround	Yes	Workaround
MS SQL	N/A	Yes	Yes	Workaround
Operational GUI	Yes	Yes	Yes	No
Reporting	Yes	Limited capacity	Yes	No
Restore to different location	Yes	Yes	Yes	Yes
Restore to individual DBs/Buckets	Yes	Yes	Yes	No
Specify retention time	Yes	Yes	Yes	Yes
Windows client	N/A	Yes	Yes	Yes

Summary

In this chapter, we discussed topics that are critical to the operation of an OpenStack cloud. We covered tactical ways to monitor, plan, and back up your cloud; this is simply the beginning. There are many great resources online that can assist you in the operation of an OpenStack cloud; however, I suggest that readers start with the actual OpenStack operations and architecture guides. These are located at `https://wiki.openstack.org/wiki/OpsGuide` and `http://docs.openstack.org/arch-design/`, respectively. These guides will provide all the required foundational information to help make operations in any cloud journey a success.

In the next chapter, you will be learning about integrating existing business and operational processes, such as identity management integration and unit testing using Jenkins.

Further reading

Please see the following for further reading relating to this chapter:

- `http://docs.openstack.org/arch/`
- `http://openstack-in-production.blogspot.com/2013/10/log-handling-and-dashboards-in-cern.html`
- `https://www.mirantis.com/validated-solution-integrations/fuel-plugins`
- `http://www.slack.com`
- `http://rally.readthedocs.io/en/latest/index.html`
- `http://developer.openstack.org/`

- http://www.nagios.com
- https://github.com/rakesh-patnaik/nagios-openstack-monitoring
- http://docs.openstack.org/ha-guide/controller-ha-haproxy.html
- https://wiki.openstack.org/wiki/CloudKitty
- http://www8.hp.com/us/en/software-solutions/capacity-planning-server-virtualization-management/
- https://access.redhat.com/documentation/en/red-hat-cloudforms/4.1/
- http://manageiq.org/
- http://talligent.com/openbook-faqs/
- https://wiki.openstack.org/wiki/Raksha
- http://www.triliodata.com/about/
- http://docs.openstack.org/ops/
- https://www.elastic.co/webinars/introduction-elk-stack

6
Integrating the Platform

One of the OpenStack architects we've worked with is fond of saying, *No OpenStack implementation is an island*. Each deployment integrates with the legacy IT infrastructure around it, from **Identity management** (**IdM**) systems to auditing systems to billing systems. OpenStack's standardized APIs make these integrations relatively simple. This chapter will cover the integration points available within an OpenStack implementation and many common integration patterns.

In this chapter, we'll look at the following points in detail:

- Identity management integration
- Provisioning workflows
- Metering and billing

These three different platform integrations demonstrate the three prominent integration patterns for OpenStack. Integrating Keystone with an IdM system such as Active Directory is relatively prescriptive—as Cinder is designed to integrate with storage arrays, Keystone is designed to integrate with IdM systems. The contract between Keystone and the IdM system is largely hidden in the code of the project.

The other two integration patterns demonstrate two different ways to interact externally with the OpenStack system. External provisioning workflows drive the OpenStack system through its REST API. They either interact directly with the Neutron, Cinder, Nova, and Glance APIs, or they leverage the Heat orchestration API to create, modify, and delete objects within the OpenStack deployment. In contrast, metering, billing, and auditing systems interact with the output of the system by either listening in on the OpenStack message bus for events to occur or by consuming events from the Event API.

IdM integration

In a 2014 blog post, OpenStack developer *Nathan Kinder* famously (and convincingly) argued that *Keystone is not an authentication service.* In this post, Kinder describes the deployment pattern of placing the Keystone service behind an Apache HTTP server, which uses native modules to perform authentication. Kinder makes two arguments in his post:

- Most people use some kind of external authentication system with OpenStack
- The reference authentication system (the SQL plugin) doesn't have any of the features that we'd expect from an authentication service

Both of these arguments have been proven in our experience; the first integration that most organizations we work with tackle is that of the IdM service.

Authentication and authorization in OpenStack

Having an understanding of how authentication and authorization work within OpenStack is helpful. Each call to an OpenStack API service is authorized by a bearer token, which is retrieved from and verified by the Keystone service. The following figure summarizes this interaction:

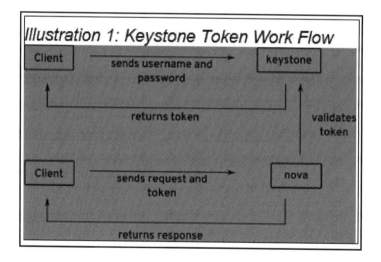

When requesting the token from Keystone, the client sends along the requested scope of the token: the tenant, project, or domain. Assuming that the credentials authorize the client, the token that Keystone returns is specific to the scope requested. Once the client has obtained the token, each API request to the other OpenStack services contains the token in an HTTP header. The other services use that token to authorize the requests from the client.

There are two versions of the Keystone API in wide use in OpenStack at present: versions 2 and 3. However, version 2 is quickly becoming deprecated. In version 2 of the API, users are authorized to specific projects or **tenants**. A user may have privileges in more than one tenant, and the privileges may vary by tenant. For example, the user **msolberg** may have administrative privileges in the msolberg tenant, but only user privileges in the **architect** tenant. Version 3 of the API introduces the concept of authorization domains, which provide a hierarchy above basic tenancy and adds the benefit of sub-tenants. Version 3 of the Keystone API has been around for a few releases, but it has taken some time for each of the services to support the new authorization model. As such, many OpenStack deployments still use the Keystone v2 API.

Keystone uses a combination of backend drivers when deciding whether to issue a token when presented with a set of credentials. The first backend driver is the identity driver. The identity driver can either be SQL (the reference implementation) or **Lightweight Directory Access Protocol** (**LDAP**). If the driver is set to LDAP, an external directory service can be used to authenticate users. The second driver is the **assignment** driver. This driver allows users to authenticate using LDAP and assign roles using the SQL database. This configuration is the most commonly used integration pattern for Active Directory.

Configuring Keystone with split assignment and identity

Before configuring Keystone to use Active Directory (or other LDAP services) for authentication, a few changes will need to be made on the Active Directory side. First, decide on mapping objects in Active Directory to the accounts in OpenStack. For example, you may want any user who has an account in the directory to have access to a tenant in OpenStack, or you may want to restrict usage to a particular group of users. If you intend to restrict users, you will need to create a group or attribute to filter them. Second, a user who has the ability to lookup on other users needs to be created. Perform a test that validates that the user has the ability to read the appropriate subtree of account objects using a utility such as `ldapsearch`. For more information on the prerequisites for the Active Directory side, refer to `https://wiki.openstack.org/wiki/HowtoIntegrateKeystonewithAD`.

Next, we will configure Keystone to use the LDAP identity backend and the SQL assignment backend. Packstack supports this configuration out of the box, and we only need to update the Hiera data on our Puppet master for our installation to reflect the new settings. The following table represents the settings that will be required:

Hiera variable	keystone.conf setting	Description
CONFIG_KEYSTONE_IDENTITY_BACKEND	identity.driver	That backend to use (ldap)
CONFIG_KEYSTONE_LDAP_URL	ldap.url	The URI for the AD LDAP service
CONFIG_KEYSTONE_LDAP_USER_DN	ldap.user	The service user for looking up accounts
CONFIG_KEYSTONE_LDAP_USER_PASSWORD	ldap.password	The password for the service user
CONFIG_KEYSTONE_LDAP_SUFFIX	ldap.suffix	The suffix for the service account
CONFIG_KEYSTONE_LDAP_USER_SUBTREE	ldap.user_tree_dn	The tree containing user accounts in AD
CONFIG_KEYSTONE_LDAP_USER_OBJECTCLASS	ldap.user_objectclass	The object class for user accounts (person)
CONFIG_KEYSTONE_LDAP_USER_FILTER	ldap.user_filter	An optional filter to use for selecting only certain users in the tree
CONFIG_KEYSTONE_LDAP_USER_ID_ATTRIBUTE	ldap.user_id_attribute	The attribute to use as the Keystone user ID (cn)
CONFIG_KEYSTONE_LDAP_USER_NAME_ATTRIBUTE	ldap.user_name_attribute	The attribute to use as the Keystone user name (cn)
CONFIG_KEYSTONE_LDAP_USER_MAIL_ATTRIBUTE	ldap.user_mail_attribute	The attribute to use as the Keystone user e-mail (mail)
CONFIG_KEYSTONE_LDAP_USER_ENABLED_ATTRIBUTE	ldap.user_enabled_attribute	The attribute that determines whether a user is enabled or not (userAccountControl)
CONFIG_KEYSTONE_LDAP_USER_ENABLED_MASK	ldap.user_enabled_mask	The bitmask to use to determine whether the account is enabled (2)
CONFIG_KEYSTONE_LDAP_USER_ENABLED_DEFAULT	ldap.user_enabled_default	The default value to use to determine whether the account is enabled (512)
CONFIG_KEYSTONE_LDAP_USER_ATTRIBUTE_IGNORE	ldap.user_attribute_ignore	Attributes to ignore on the object (password, tenant_id, tenants)
CONFIG_KEYSTONE_LDAP_USER_ALLOW_CREATE	ldap.user_allow_create	Whether or not we can create users (False)
CONFIG_KEYSTONE_LDAP_USER_ALLOW_UPDATE	ldap.user_allow_update	Whether or not we can update users (False)
CONFIG_KEYSTONE_LDAP_USER_ALLOW_DELETE	ldap.user_allow_delete	Whether or not we can delete users (False)

Once the appropriate settings have been determined for your environment, update `/etc/puppet/heiradata/defaults.yaml` with them. On the next Puppet run, Keystone will be reconfigured to use Active Directory for authentication.

As we mentioned before, the method of having Keystone authenticate users against LDAP is being phased out in favor of having the Apache HTTP server perform the authentication itself and then pass through a `REMOTE_USER` environment variable. By default, Packstack will provision Keystone as a **Web Server Gateway Interface** (**WSGI**) service within Apache. Configuring the Keystone virtual host to authenticate users is described at `http://docs.openstack.org/developer/keystone/external-auth.html`.

Provisioning workflows

We've spent almost the entirety of this book discussing how to implement OpenStack and very little of it discussing how most organizations are actually using it. In this section, we'll explore different ways that OpenStack adopters typically provision virtual infrastructure. First, we'll look at giving users access to the Horizon user interface. Then, we'll look at provisioning through the Nova, Cinder, and Neutron APIs. Finally, we'll look at using Heat to orchestrate the OpenStack infrastructure using templates.

The Horizon user interface

The Horizon dashboard UI provides an intuitive and standardized interface for users who already understand the concepts of cloud computing and want to have complete control over their provisioned infrastructure. The dashboard works particularly well in situations where the end user is expected to provide some level of support, where they are responsible for scheduling their own backups, for example. We've seen this approach used in public web hosting companies and also in private cloud use cases where the primary goal is to provide low-cost compute environments to development teams.

Organizations that provide access to the dashboard to their end users will typically customize it to some extent. The appearance of the dashboard is relatively insignificant to customize. The Liberty release of OpenStack introduced the concept of **themes** for Horizon, which provides a standardized way of changing colors, images, and layouts. There is also a simple mechanism for enabling or disabling the various panels on the dashboard.

Finally, it is also possible to override the Python classes that correspond to the panels by means of a **customization module**. We've seen organizations do this when they want to gather additional information from users when they're provisioning infrastructure. Information on the various options is available at `https://docs.openstack.org/horizon/latest/configuration/customizing.html`.

The following screenshot represents the Horizon dashboard UI:

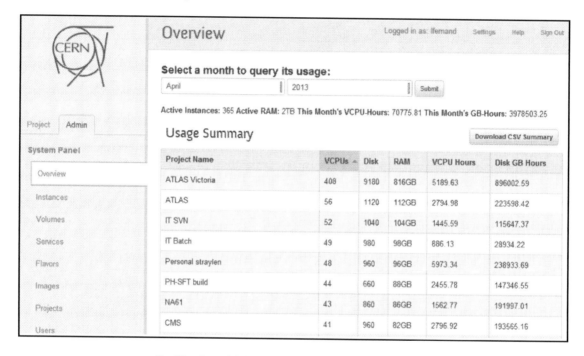

Conseil Européen pour la Recherche Nucléaire (CERN)customized OpenStack dashboard

Although creating a custom theme for the Horizon dashboard is relatively simple and is probably a prerequisite for organizations that are going to provide access to their end users, overriding the classes that make up the dashboard is a relatively expensive option to pursue. Although the initial development may not be that difficult, it introduces a support burden in the longer term. It also adds additional testing requirements that are difficult to automate. For these reasons, organizations that want to tailor the provisioning process to their specific goals will typically use an external service catalog, which interacts with the API on behalf of the end users.

Using REST APIs

OpenStack REST APIs are patterned after the Amazon EC2 APIs and are simple to interact with. There are typically two options for this interaction, depending on the language that the provisioning system is written in. Clients can either call the APIs directly using the language's HTTP or REST library or they can use one of the many **cloud libraries** that have sprung up in the past few years. These libraries can greatly simplify development by taking care of the authentication and serialization pieces of the work, but they can also limit the available API actions. Cloud libraries that we've seen commonly used these days include Apache jclouds for Java, OpenStack Shade for Python, and Fog for Ruby.

In this chapter, we'll interact directly with the REST APIs. Let's break down how a virtual instance would be launched using the REST API:

1. The client requests a token from Keystone
2. The client retrieves a list of keypairs from Nova
3. The client retrieves a list of images from Nova
4. The client retrieves a list of flavors from Nova
5. The client retrieves a list of networks from Neutron
6. The client optionally creates a volume in Cinder
7. The client asks Nova to create an instance with the selected image, flavor, network, and (optionally) volume

The client can then perform various actions on the instance when created, including termination. Let's walk through this workflow using the Python requests library:

1. First, we'll request a token from Keystone (the actual Python code is as follows):

```
import requests #http://docs.python-requests.org/en/latest
import json

KEYSTONE_URL = 'http://controller:5000/v2.0/'
TENANT      = 'demo'
USERNAME    = 'demo'
PASSWORD    = 'secret'

r = requests.post("%s/tokens"% (KEYSTONE_URL,), json={
  "auth": {
    "tenantName": TENANT,
    "passwordCredentials": {
      "username": USERNAME,
      "password": PASSWORD,
    }
```

```
    }
  })

  if r.ok:
    token = r.json()['access']['token']['id']
  else:
    raise Exception(r.text)
```

2. The requests library simplifies working with the REST interface a little by deserializing the JSON returned by Keystone into a Python dictionary through the `json()` function. The response from Keystone contains the token ID, which we will include as a header to any further requests:

```
# Place the token in the X-Auth-Token header
headers = {'X-Auth-Token': token}
```

3. The response from Keystone also contains a service catalog, a set of links to the other services that we want to interact with. Keystone may give out links for more than one region, depending on the configuration. In our lab, though, we can just use the first link for each service. The following code will search the catalog for the compute and network services:

```
# Find the link to the Nova API in the service catalog:
for service in r.json()['access']['serviceCatalog']:
  if service['type'] == 'compute':
    nova_endpoint = service['endpoints'][0]['publicURL']
  if service['type'] == 'network':
    neutron_endpoint = service['endpoints'][0]['publicURL']
```

Note that, the endpoint in the catalog is scoped to the tenant we authenticated with. For example, if our tenant ID is 8ce08c9fa6c54ba094be743a55dc5b9a, our Nova endpoint will be http://10.3.71.50:8774/v2/8ce08c9fa6c54ba094be743a55dc5b9a. As such, the only endpoint that shouldn't be dynamically determined is the Keystone endpoint. All other endpoints that need to be interacted with should be pulled from the service catalog.

4. Next, we'll look up the keypair, image, flavor, and network to use when launching the image:

```
keypair_ref = None
# Get the list of available keypairs:
keypairs = requests.get("%s/os-keypairs"% nova_endpoint,
headers=headers)
# take the first one
```

```
keypair_ref = keypairs.json()['keypairs'][0]['keypair']['name']

image_ref = None
# Get the list of available images:
images = requests.get("%s/images"% nova_endpoint,
headers=headers)
# Select the "cirros" image:
for image in images.json()['images']:
    if image['name'] == 'cirros':
        image_ref = image['id']

flavor_ref = None
# Get the list of available flavors:
flavors = requests.get("%s/flavors"% nova_endpoint,
headers=headers)
# Select the "m1.small" flavor
for flavor in flavors.json()['flavors']:
    if flavor['name'] == 'm1.small':
        flavor_ref = flavor['id']

network_ref = None
# Get the list of available networks:
networks = requests.get("%s/v2.0/networks"% neutron_endpoint,
headers=headers)
# Select the "private" network
for network in networks.json()['networks']:
    if network['name'] == 'private':
        network_ref = network['id']
```

Each of these GET requests includes the token that we retrieved from Keystone in the headers. The keypair and flavor are retrieved from the Nova API, as is the image, although it is actually stored in Glance. The network reference is also available from the Nova API, but we retrieve it from the Neutron API in this example. The Neutron API provides more information and control over the network objects.

Note that while the Nova endpoint includes a version string (v2), the Neutron endpoint does not. Also, note that the Neutron endpoint does not include the tenant ID. Each OpenStack API was developed independently by different teams, and there is little consistency between them.

5. The following code will launch an instance using the four references we retrieved in the previous section:

```
# Launch the instance:
server = requests.post("%s/servers"% (nova_endpoint,), json={
```

```
"server": {
  "name": "new_server",
  "imageRef": image_ref,
  "flavorRef": flavor_ref,
  "key_name": keypair_ref,
  "networks": [{
    "uuid": network_ref
  }]
  }
},
headers=headers)
server_ref = server.json()['server']['id']
```

The preceding behavior is normal for the REST API; this is a POST request with JSON. There are a couple of things to note about this call. The first is that the call blocks only as long as it takes for the Nova scheduler to accept the request. A successful return code does not mean that the instance was successfully launched. The second is that the JSON returned by the API is not a serialized representation of the server object. Instead, it provides a set of links to the representation of the object. The link to the object comprises the API version, the tenant ID, the string servers, and the instance ID. For example, http://192.168.0.10:8774/v2/8ce08c9fa6c54ba094be743a55dc5b9a/servers/d87f6e9d-347e-48f3-acfb-6f2e85c43629. The following request provides the status of the instance:

```
requests.get(server.json()['server']['links'][0]['href'],
headers=headers)
```

6. Once an instance has been created, actions can be POSTed to the instance's URL with the string action appended. For example, the following code will stop an instance:

```
server_url = server.json()['server']['links'][0]['href']
stop = requests.post("%s/action"% (server_url,), json={
  "os-stop": None
}, headers=headers)
```

7. Finally, to delete an instance, issue an HTTP DELETE request to the server's URL:

```
delete = requests.delete(server_url, headers=headers)
```

As with any of the request responses in this example, the HTTP status code indicates the success or failure of the request. The successful status code for the delete request is 204 and the successful status code for an action is typically 202. More information on expected status codes, request parameters, and response parameters is available in the Compute API documentation at http://developer.openstack.org/api-ref-compute-v2.1.html.

Provisioning with templates

The end users of the service catalogs that drive the provisioning workflows for software-defined infrastructures tend to be application developers. Allowing developers to provision networks, volumes, and instances through APIs is extremely useful for automated continuous integration builds and deployments. Although there are a number of advantages to this approach, many organizations would prefer to let their developers provision environments made up of these elements instead. First off, the number of options exposed either in the API or in the Horizon dashboard is pretty impressive. A typical deployment will have at least two or three flavors, four or five images, private and public networks, arbitrary volume sizes, and so on. Choosing from all of these options to just launch an instance is time-consuming. It can also put a burden on the team that has to support them. Once software-defined networking is introduced, the end user may be expected to understand networking, routing, and load balancing in order to provision a working system. This is really unrealistic in most enterprise environments.

The solution to managing the complexity of software-defined infrastructure is to compose a service catalog of templates. These templates can be made up of single instances or multiple instances, rich or simple network topologies, and highly customized or standard images.

The orchestration API is much simpler to program to as well. Let's walk through an example:

1. We begin in the same way as the previous example, by requesting a token from Keystone:

```
import requests #http://docs.python-requests.org/en/latest
import json

KEYSTONE_URL = 'http://controller01:5000/v2.0/'
TENANT       = 'demo'
USERNAME     = 'demo'
PASSWORD     = 'secret'

r = requests.post("%s/tokens"% (KEYSTONE_URL,), json={
    "auth": {
```

```
      "tenantName": TENANT,
      "passwordCredentials": {
        "username": USERNAME,
        "password": PASSWORD,
      }
    }
})

if r.ok:
  token = r.json()['access']['token']['id']
else:
  raise Exception(r.text)

# Place the token in the X-Auth-Token header
headers = {'X-Auth-Token': token}
```

2. Then, instead of searching for the Compute API, we'll search for the endpoint of the Orchestration service:

```
# Find the link to the Heat API in the service catalog:
for service in r.json()['access']['serviceCatalog']:
  if service['type'] == 'orchestration':
    heat_endpoint = service['endpoints'][0]['publicURL']
```

The Heat URL, like the Nova URL, contains the UUID of the tenant.

3. Finally, we POST the JSON string representing the Heat template to the service:

```
stack = requests.post("%s/stacks"% (heat_endpoint,), json={
  "stack_name": "new_server",
  "template": {
    "heat_template_version": "2013-05-23",
    "resources": {
      "new_server_port": {
        "type": "OS::Neutron::Port",
        "properties": {
          "network": "private"
        }
      },
      "new_server": {
        "type": "OS::Nova::Server",
        "properties": {
          "key_name": "demo",
          "flavor": "m1.small",
          "image": "cirros",
          "networks": [ {
            "port": {
              "get_resource": "new_server_port"
```

```
                        }
                     } ]
                  }
               }
            }
         }
      }
   }, headers=headers)
```

Heat performs the name-to-ID translations for us, so we don't need to look up the reference for the flavor, image, key, or network. The response to the call contains the status code (`201` is success) and a link to the (`stack.json()['stack']['links'][0]['href']`) `stack` `object`. The Heat API exposes an `actions` link similar to the Compute API. Stacks may be suspended and resumed via that mechanism.

Perhaps the most important feature of the Heat API, though, is the ability to reference an external template. To use this feature, use the `template_url` attribute instead of specifying a template. Observe the following example:

```
stack = requests.post("%s/stacks"% (heat_endpoint,), json={
   "stack_name": "new_server",
   "template_url": "http://www.example.com/heat-
   templates/new_server.yaml"
}, headers=headers)
```

The templates can then be separated from the provisioning code. This allows them to reside in separate version control repositories and allows different teams to work on the catalog and the provisioning logic out of step.

Almost every object that can be created via OpenStack APIs can be orchestrated using Heat. For more information on heat templates, refer to the Heat Template Guide at `http://docs.openstack.org/developer/heat/template_guide/`.

Metering and billing

Whether you're building a public cloud or a private cloud, one of the most critical capabilities of the system is tracking the usage of the virtual objects that are provisioned by the users or tenants. Usage in OpenStack is tracked largely in the same way it is in Amazon Web Services. For compute resources, the system tracks when a particular instance was started and when it was terminated. The cost of a compute resource is associated with the number of CPU cores or the amount of memory in the flavor associated with the instance. Some organizations may also associate a cost with the image as well.

For example, an instantiation of a Red Hat Enterprise Linux image may cost a certain number of cents per hour, whereas an instantiation of a Microsoft Windows image may cost something different. Other resources may be billed based on when they're provisioned regardless of use. For example, a tenant might be charged for how long a floating IP was assigned to the project, regardless of whether it was attached to an instance. Cinder volumes are frequently treated this way.

Whether your organization intends to charge your customers based on consumption or your organization intends to just show your customers their consumption, there are a few different strategies for tracking and reporting usage data. Some organizations that provision resources onto OpenStack through the API by a service catalog choose to use the service catalog implementation as the system of record. This helps maintain consistency for the user. For example, if they've provisioned a three tier-application, they probably want to be billed for a three-tier application and not for three virtual machines, a Cinder volume, and a floating IP. For PaaS or Continuous Integration use cases, though, the total amount of compute and storage used over a period of time is probably more important.

There are a few basic approaches to tracking usage in OpenStack. Systems can listen for events on the message bus or query Ceilometer for them and then extrapolate usage data. Systems can also query Ceilometer directly for usage data. Each of these approaches is also useful for other use cases than metering and billing and some are better suited than others for each of them. For example, listening and timing events can offer great insights into the performance of a system. Also, compliance workflows may be driven by certain events within the OpenStack system.

Listening to OpenStack

There are two modes of internal communication in the OpenStack system. The first is to GET or POST to the REST API, and the second is to pull and push messages onto the message queue. Each of the services uses a combination of each; when the Nova API gets a request to provision a resource over the REST API, it passes that request along to the compute nodes via the message bus. They send back usage data over the bus, but they use the API to communicate with other services. These two modes of communication are also available for integration. Just as we can provision resources using the REST API, we can track their progress using the message bus.

The following code example uses the Kombu library in Python to attach to the Nova queue on the message bus to listen for these RPC calls between the various Nova services. First, we define a callback method to be used to process events on the bus. This simple method just prints the body of the message:

```
from kombu import Connection, Exchange, Queue

def process_message(body, message):
  print body
  message.ack()
```

Then, we create a queue named `listener` and bind it to the `nova` exchange. In the following example, we're going to subscribe to all messages on the `nova` queue:

```
nova_exchange = Exchange('nova', 'topic', durable=False)
nova_queue    = Queue('listener', exchange = nova_exchange,
routing_key='#')
conn = Connection('amqp://guest:guest@192.168.0.10//')
consumer = conn.Consumer(nova_queue, callbacks=[process_message])
consumer.consume()
```

> Note that the `connection` string is specific to the deployment in question. The username and password for the message bus should align with the settings in `/etc/nova/nova.conf`.

Finally, we'll check the queue for messages and process them:

```
while True:
  conn.drain_events()
```

Running this example will show just how chatty the Nova services are. The message format for these RPC messages is well defined, but the content of the messages is version-specific. For these reasons, most developers will choose to use the notification subsystem instead.

Using the notification subsystem

Each of the OpenStack services can be configured to emit notifications on the message bus. These notifications can then be picked up by messaging clients or by the Ceilometer service. Notifications were originally implemented by each service separately, but the functionality has been folded into the Oslo Messaging library as a common interface.

To enable notification in Nova, the following settings need to be changed in `/etc/nova/nova.conf`:

nova.conf Setting	Example value	Description
`instance_usage_audit`	`true`	Turns on usage auditing
`instance_usage_audit_period`	`hour`	Sets usage auditing to hourly
`notify_on_state_change`	`vm_and_task_state`	Tells Nova to send a notification when a VM's state changes
`notification_driver`	`messagingv2`	Tells Nova to send notifications to the message bus

Other notification drivers are available as well. Notifications can be sent to syslog, for example. For more information, refer to the Oslo Messaging FAQ at `http://docs.openstack.org/developer/oslo.messaging/FAQ.html`.

A simple client that can listen to these notification events is provided here:

```python
#!/usr/bin/env python

from kombu import Connection, Exchange, Queue

def process_message(body, message):
  print body
  message.ack()

nova_exchange = Exchange('nova', 'topic', durable=False)
notifications_queue    = Queue('notification-listener', exchange =
nova_exchange, routing_key='notifications.info')
conn = Connection('amqp://guest:guest@192.168.0.10//')
consumer = conn.Consumer(notifications_queue, callbacks=[process_message])
consumer.consume()

while True:
  conn.drain_events()
```

This example creates a queue named `notification-listener`, which is bound to the `nova` exchange. Instead of listening to all events on the exchange, though, we subscribe to the `notifications.info` topic. This ensures that we receive only the messages that are designated as notifications by the Nova service.

A higher-level abstraction, which can be used by Python programmers who are interacting with OpenStack, can be found in the `oslo.messaging` library. Documentation on this approach is available at `http://docs.openstack.org/developer/oslo.messaging/notification_listener.html`. Another option is to use the Yagi library (`https://github.com/rackerlabs/yagi`), which is in turn used by Stack Tach from Rackspace (`https://github.com/openstack/stacktach`).

Consuming events from Ceilometer

Consuming events from the message queue allows for a push-style integration model in the OpenStack environment. Writing and maintaining a daemon to consume events from the queue and act on them can be onerous for many organizations, though. A much simpler option is to poll the Ceilometer interface for events over the REST API. Given that Nova (as well as other services) is configured to emit notifications over the message bus, the Ceilometer service can store them and make them available for polling. To enable this functionality, set `store_events` to `True` in `/etc/ceilometer/ceilometer.conf`.

The following example shows how to retrieve events from Ceilometer using the Python requests library:

1. First, we begin by retrieving a token from Keystone:

```
import requests #http://docs.python-requests.org/en/latest
import json

KEYSTONE_URL = 'http://controller01:5000/v2.0/'
TENANT       = 'demo'
USERNAME     = 'demo'
PASSWORD     = 'secret'

r = requests.post("%s/tokens"% (KEYSTONE_URL,), json={
  "auth": {
    "tenantName": TENANT,
    "passwordCredentials": {
      "username": USERNAME,
      "password": PASSWORD,
    }
  }
})
if r.ok:
  token = r.json()['access']['token']['id']
else:
  raise Exception(r.text)
```

```
# Place the token in the X-Auth-Token header
headers = {'X-Auth-Token': token}
```

2. Then, we find the `metering` service in Keystone's catalog:

```
# Find the link to the Ceilometer API in the service catalog:
for service in r.json()['access']['serviceCatalog']:
  if service['type'] == 'metering':
    metering_endpoint = service['endpoints'][0]['publicURL']
```

3. Finally, we request all available events using a GET request and print out the types:

```
events = requests.get("%s/v2/events"% (metering_endpoint,),
headers=headers)

for e in events.json():
  print e['event_type']
```

The GET request can contain filters for certain types of event and can contain a limit to the number of events to retrieve. For more information on using the Ceilometer Event API, refer to http://docs.openstack.org/developer/ceilometer/webapi/v2.html.

Reading meters in Ceilometer

In the preceding sections, we walked through different methods for retrieving event data from an OpenStack cloud. This event data can then be used to track usage and generate billing information for end users of the system. The Ceilometer service was designed to do exactly that: track usage based on event data and generate billing information. Ceilometer makes this data available through a REST API.

The following example uses the Python requests library to request the duration of instances running within the user's tenant:

1. First, we begin by requesting a token from Keystone:

```
#!/usr/bin/env python

import requests #http://docs.python-requests.org/en/latest
import json

KEYSTONE_URL = 'http://controller01:5000/v2.0/'
TENANT       = 'demo'
USERNAME     = 'demo'
PASSWORD     = 'secret'
```

```
r = requests.post("%s/tokens"% (KEYSTONE_URL,), json={
  "auth": {
    "tenantName": TENANT,
    "passwordCredentials": {
      "username": USERNAME,
      "password": PASSWORD,
    }
  }
})

if r.ok:
  token = r.json()['access']['token']['id']
else:
  raise Exception(r.text)

# Place the token in the X-Auth-Token header
headers = {'X-Auth-Token': token}
```

2. Then, we get the link to the Ceilometer service from the service catalog:

```
# Find the link to the Ceilometer API in the service catalog:
for service in r.json()['access']['serviceCatalog']:
  if service['type'] == 'metering':
    metering_endpoint = service['endpoints'][0]['publicURL']
```

3. Next, we issue a GET request for the statistics for the `Meter` instance. Ceilometer comes with a set of predefined meters for things such as instance run time, CPU usage, and disk usage:

```
tenant_id = r.json()['access']['token']['tenant']['id']
filter = {'q.field': 'project', 'q.value': tenant_id}
statistics = requests.get("%s/v2/meters/instance/statistics"%
(metering_endpoint,), headers=headers)
```

For a full list of available meters, refer to `http://docs.openstack.org/admin-guide-cloud/telemetry-measurements.html`.

> Note that we've scoped the request for statistics to our own tenant with a search filter. A call that generates a billing statement for each tenant would iterate through the list of tenants and gather the usage for each of them. It would also be scoped to a period of time with an additional filter. More information on filters is available at `http://docs.openstack.org/developer/ceilometer/webapi/v2.html`.

The JSON returned by the call contains a list of statistics. We're interested in the `duration` value:

```
print statistics.json()[0]['duration']
```

Other statistics are available for meters such as `sums`, `averages`, `minimums`, and `maximums`.

Introducing OpenStack Gnocchi

Since the OpenStack Ocata release, the ceilometer time series database has been replaced with a number of projects. Gnocchi, a former OpenStack project, is a time series database that uses high-performance data structures to store large quantities of metrics in an aggregated manner. OpenStack project Panko replaces Ceilometer functionality and alerts are now delivered through Aodh.

Since this section is about meters and measures we will be discussing only Gnocchi. Gnocchi uses two different backends for storing data: one to storing the time series (the storage driver) and one for indexing the resources (the index driver). The backend for storing meters can be one of many different storage formats. These include file, Ceph, S3 (Swift/AWS S3), and even Redis. Gnocchi, like most other OpenStack projects, can be accessed via REST API:

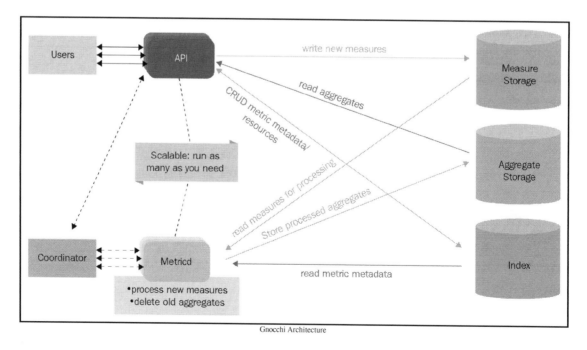

Gnocchi Architecture

Contrary to Ceilometer and other time-series databases, the services under Gnocchi are horizontally scalable. If the load increases, one cloud simply scale the number of daemons to handle more requests into Gnocchi. Lack of scaling ability was one of the largest complaints about the Ceilometer/MongoDB combination as referenced in many OpenStack user surveys.

If you are installing an OpenStack version from Ocata forward, Gnocchi will automatically be included in the install. If you are installing older versions of OpenStack (Mitaka to Ocata), there are ways to convert or replace Ceilometer's dependence on MongoDB and convert to Gnocchi. It is rather trivial to install Gnocchi on any system, it is as simple as the command:

```
pip install gnocchi [postgresql, ceph, keystone]
```

This would install Gnocchi with PostgreSQL, Ceph for storage and Keystone for authentication. There are a list of variations to this install procedure listed at `https://gnocchi.xyz/install.html`.

Gnocchi runs as a standalone http server that services the `gnocchi-api` and `gnocchi-metricd` daemons. It can also be run via WSGI like other OpenStack services through Apache's `mod_wsgi`.

To configure how Gnocci's metrics are aggregated and stored, the archive policies must be defined. However, there are four default policies defined on install or upgrade. Each archive policy definition is expressed as the number of points over a time span. If your archive policy defines a policy of 10 points with a granularity of 1 second, the time series archive will keep up to 10 seconds, each representing an aggregation over 1 second. This means the time series will at maximum retain 10 seconds of data between the more recent point and the oldest point. This does not mean that it will be 10 consecutive seconds: there might be a gap if data is fed irregularly.

More information on archive policies can be found at the Gnocchi documentation at `https://gnocchi.xyz/rest.html#archive-policy-rule`.

Basically, Gnocchi's function is to serve metrics via API (measures) and then preaggregate this data based on archive policies using `gnocchi-metricd`. Furthermore, Gnocchi is able to index large aggregate information from regions, clouds, and infrastructures and combine if for delivery.

Updating the design document

In this chapter, we've identified several different ways to interact with OpenStack using the available APIs. Now it is a good time to revisit the design document and fill out the **Requirements** section. An ideal set of requirements for an OpenStack cloud will have the following characteristics:

- Each requirement should be atomic to limit the scope of the requirement
- Each requirement should the contain context; there should be information on who will be using the functionality and under what circumstances
- Each requirement should be testable, ideally in an automated fashion

If these conditions are met, we can generate policy documentation based on the principle that roles should have access to that functionality and we can generate automated test suites that verify that the requirements of the platform are met. These test suites can in turn be used in monitoring suites to ensure that the running system is performing according to specification.

Writing requirements

In this section, we'll look at some example requirements. As we saw earlier in the chapter, every interaction with the OpenStack REST APIs starts with a request to Keystone for a token. The following user story is a good representation of that interaction:

> *"As an End User of the system, I should be able to present my Active Directory username and password to the Keystone service and receive a token that authorizes me to use other OpenStack services. This token will be scoped to the projects to which I have been granted access by the OpenStack Administrator."*

The following metadata can be associated with this requirement:

- **User**: End user
- **Inputs**: Active Directory authentication credentials
- **Outputs**: Authorization token and Project scope

We can then also describe an implementation of the requirement using the REST API:

```
POST /v2.0/tokens
{
  "auth": {
    "tenantName": "demo",
    "passwordCredentials": {
```

```
      "username": "demo",
      "password": "secret"
    }
  }
}
RESPONSE 200
{
  "access": {
    "token": {
      "issued_at": "2014-01-30T15:30:58.819584",
      "expires": "2014-01-31T15:30:58Z",
      "id": "aaaaa-bbbbb-ccccc-dddd",
      "tenant": {
        "description": null,
        "enabled": true,
        "id": "fc394f2ab2df4114bde39905f800dc57",
        "name": "demo"
      }
    },
  }
}
```

If we wanted to, we could also identify the service-level agreement for this requirement. For example, we could specify that the Keystone service should respond within 10 seconds with a valid token. This could be used to establish acceptable performance thresholds for the system.

Let's walk through a more complex example, that of launching an instance:

"As an End User of the system, I should be able to present my Keystone token and instantiate a given image as a virtual machine via the Nova API. I should be able to specify the image, the flavor, an SSH key, a private network, and metadata for the instance."

The following metadata can be associated with this requirement:

- **User**: End user
- **Inputs**: Keystone token, compute service API, tenant ID, image ID, flavor ID, SSH key name, network ID, and metadata keys and values
- **Outputs**: Instance description

An example of this requirement is as follows:

```
POST /v2.1/{tenant_id}/servers
{
  "server": {
```

```
      "name": "example-server",
      "imageRef": "{image_id}",
      "flavorRef": "{flavor_id}",
      "key_name": "{key_name}"
      "networks": "{"uuid": "{network_id}"}"
      "metadata": {
        "{metadata_key}": "{metadata_value}"
      }
    }
  }
}
RESPONSE 202
{
  "server": {
    "id": "{server_id}",
    "links": [
    {
      "href": "/v2.1/{tenant_id}/servers/{server_id}",
      "rel": "self"
    },
    {
      "href": "/servers/{server_id}",
      "rel": "bookmark"
    }
    ],
  }
}
```

Note that we've kept the requirement relatively simple. We could have walked through the whole call and response script leading up to the final call, but that's really better served in the test implementation. We'll walk through how to translate requirements into tests in the next section.

Testing requirements

In Chapter 4, *Building the Deployment Pipeline*, we wrote some basic tests for our OpenStack deployment using shell tools. In this section, we'll combine the code examples discussed earlier in the chapter with the Python unit test library to generate a set of automated tests that can be run from Jenkins to verify our deployment. The following example, which uses the Python unittest and requests libraries, is very simple, but can be used as a starting point:

```
#!/usr/bin/env python

import unittest
import requests #http://docs.python-requests.org/en/latest
```

```
import json

KEYSTONE_URL = 'http://controller01:5000/v2.0/'
TENANT       = 'demo'
USERNAME     = 'demo'
PASSWORD     = 'secret'
```

Once we've imported the necessary libraries and set the global variables, we'll create a `TestCase` object for our tests:

```
class TestKeystone(unittest.TestCase):
"""Set of Keystone-specific tests"""
```

Any function whose name begins with `test` will be treated as a test to be run by the `unittest` library. We'll define a function that exercises the REST call described in the first user story:

```
def test_001_get_token(self):
"""Requirement 001: Authorization Token"""
r = requests.post("%s/tokens"% (KEYSTONE_URL,), json={
  "auth": {
    "tenantName": TENANT,
    "passwordCredentials": {
      "username": USERNAME,
      "password": PASSWORD,
    }
  }
})
if r.ok:
  self.assertEqual(r.status_code, 200)
  token = r.json()['access']['token']['id']
  self.assertTrue(token)
else:
  raise Exception(r.text)
```

This test is based on the examples that we used earlier in this chapter to retrieve a token from the `Keystone` service. We've added two assertion statements that verify the service is responding the way we've designed it. The first asserts that the response code is 200, and the second asserts that the JSON response contains a value for the token.

To enable the test to be run from the command line, we add a call to the `unittest` library at the end of the script:

```
if __name__ == '__main__':
  unittest.main()
```

If we check this script into the `test` directory of the code repository we created in `Chapter 4`, *Building the Deployment Pipeline,* we can call this automated test by running the script from Jenkins. Each requirement in the design document should have an automated test associated with it in this fashion. As requirements are added to the design document and implemented in Puppet, new tests that represent them can be added to the suite.

Summary

In this chapter, we looked at three integration patterns within the OpenStack platform. The first pattern was to use the built-in integration functionality provided by Keystone to integrate with Active Directory. The second was to use the REST APIs to provision infrastructure into the OpenStack environment. The third was to listen in on the message bus for notifications. Once we had explored the various ways that we can interact with the system, we wrote requirements for our deployed system in the design document with them in mind. Finally, these requirements were translated into automated tests that could be inserted into the deployment pipeline.

Some organizations that we worked with expressed frustration at the complexity of integrating the OpenStack platform with the other services in their environment. For these organizations, a **Cloud Management Platform** (**CMP**) that obfuscates some of the technical details of integration is an option worth considering. CMPs, such as Red Hat's CloudForms or Dell's Cloud Manager, will wire into the REST APIs and the message bus of an OpenStack implementation and allow higher-level access to the objects within the virtual infrastructure. They also offer out-of-the-box integrations with third-party authentication, service catalogs, and billing systems.

We like to think of the entire OpenStack system as a massive integration platform. Before OpenStack, organizations spent huge amounts of resources integrating their storage, network, and compute infrastructure with their organizational infrastructure. The open design of the system is one of its greatest strengths. In the next chapter, we will be discussing OpenStack security. We will examine common security practices, such as logging, patching, and encryption, as well as some application security suggestions.

Further reading

Please refer to the following links for further reading:

- **Keystone is not an authentication service, Nathan Kinder**: `https://blog-nkinder.rhcloud.com/?p=130`
- **How to Integrate Keystone with Active Directory**: `https://wiki.openstack.org/wiki/HowtoIntegrateKeystonewithAD`
- **Customizing Horizon**: `http://docs.openstack.org/developer/horizon/topics/customizing.html`
- **OpenStack API Documentation**: `http://developer.openstack.org/api-guide/quick-start/index.html`

7
Securing the Cloud

As more companies have begun to bring OpenStack out of the development environments and into production (refer to the following chart), real concerns about security are taking priority. This chapter will not only help outline some best practices about the OpenStack infrastructure security, but also highlight how OpenStack users and operators can bring the same level of legacy security to workloads that run on top of OpenStack clouds. The following chart show the results from the 2017 (June-December) OpenStack User Survey:

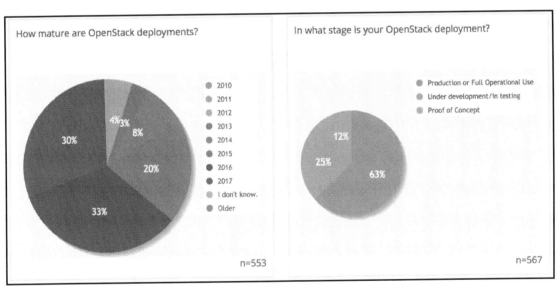

In this chapter, we will cover the following:

- Security zones within OpenStack
- Software vulnerabilities
- Hardening hypervisors

Security zones within OpenStack

Within an OpenStack deployment, there exists a series of logical security zones. These are the basic areas of trust within the OpenStack platform that can be leveraged by applications, servers, networks, or users. These zones have an increasing level of trust and can be broken down into the following zones:

- **Public zones**: These zones within OpenStack are an entirely untrusted areas of a cloud's infrastructure. By convention, they are the most open and are thus called public. They are not necessarily open to the internet, but the area is open to being consumed by untrusted resources and on networks without the operators direct authority. This area requires encryption and other compensating controls in order to meet the security requirements of most organizations.

- **Guest zones**: These zones are for instances that are provisioned within the OpenStack cloud. They include inter-tenant network instance traffic (one instance to another across segregated networks or traffic on the same tenant network). This traffic is not the traffic that supports the infrastructure of the cloud services and provides the API access to OpenStack's native RESTful API endpoints. Providing unregulated public IP addresses into instances that reside in this domain will cause the domain to be untrusted. The only way this area can be considered trusted is when the compensating controls have been implemented to regulate public IP access into this zone using external network controls.

- **Management zones**: These are the zones where the OpenStack services reside and interact. These particular zones are typically isolated for OpenStack control plane traffic only. Due to the sensitive nature of this internal communication, steps must be taken to harden this particular network, and access to this network should only be given to the servers that are operating the control plane for OpenStack. Once this is done, this zone is considered trusted. In any case, where this zone is made to be routed or connected to a routable network, in effect bridging it to an untrusted zone, this network immediately becomes untrusted and must have compensating controls implemented immediately. This zone is particularly sensitive to network latency and capacity. Best practices dictate that this zone be used expressly for OpenStack management traffic.

- **Data zones**: These are the security zones that primarily contain the services and network traffic pertaining to the storage and file sharing services within OpenStack. This data typically requires high security and high levels of confidentiality. The level of trust in this network zone is highly dependent on the workloads running in the cloud and the type of deployment that is done. Therefore, this zone can be trusted or untrusted, and without knowing the specifics of the type of deployment, we cannot assign a default level of trust. It is important to understand these zones when considering OpenStack security and the resources and services running on the platform. Developers have purposely segregated access to varying parts of the platform to segregate privileged and nonprivileged zones as well as to reduce cross-zone attacks. This zone is traffic-intensive and should not be shared with any other zone for security and performance reasons.

Software vulnerabilities

OpenStack is an orchestration platform written mostly in Python and runs on top of Linux-based operating systems. This orchestration platform is responsible for provisioning instances or Infrastructure as a Service to tenants in support of workloads that are required to run in a cloud environment. Therefore, OpenStack software vulnerabilities can be broken down into two main groups. The first group consists of containers, instances, or bare metal servers that OpenStack provisions and orchestrates; the second group consists of the OpenStack infrastructure environment and its hosts.

Instance software security and patching

Under OpenStack, the hypervisor creates and runs independent virtual machines or instances. These instances require software updates and patching separate from the underlying OpenStack infrastructure on which it resides. Updates to the hypervisor and underlying server operating systems do not propagate up to the active workloads and instances; therefore, two strategies must exist—one for instances running on the cloud and another for the cloud infrastructure.

The instance strategy should align with the existing organizational and governance policies that are currently in effect that control patching of existing legacy systems. Because OpenStack launches instances based on images and flavors that may have executable metadata injected into the instance upon boot, there are multiple ways to ensure that the latest hardened image is used prior to launching an instance depending on the workload type.

For the traditional, ephemeral type workloads commonly found on OpenStack clouds, regular updates to images in Glance should be performed as per organizational policy and should be controlled by a trusted organization within a company. These updates should add patches and security fixes to an operating system and be imported as an existing image in the glance repository. Images can also be enabled for signature verification to further ensure file integrity. These updated images should be tested in a lower development or sandbox environment before implementing into production. The images will then serve as the base production operating systems for any new instances using that image. However, the running images on existing instances will not change. The security patches will not take effect until the instances are rebooted. Typically, ephemeral workloads tend to be able to reboot without impacting the availability of the application based on cloud native design; however, persistent workloads running on the cloud will need to develop application-based strategies in order to maintain uptime of the application while patching. Some organizations have strict rules governing the rebooting of instances running on old versions of images depending on whether the patch applied to the image was for security or simply an update.

Default OpenStack security policies should be created to allow legacy software compliance tools to scan hosts for software update compliance. In the case of persistent workloads and instances not experiencing frequent reboots or instances that need to maintain certain levels of availability, security policies may be created to allow these instances to use legacy software repository-based patching solutions and implement patches in a traditional fashion by patching the running instance. However, there may be additional network configurations needed to make the software repositories available within tenant networks based on an organization's OpenStack network deployment. For both the ephemeral and persistent workloads, `cloud-init` and `cloudbase-init` could be used to execute an update to an image upon boot using native software management tools and the local software repositories. However, these updates that may only occur upon boot may also delay provisioning depending on the number of updates performed on the image. This is why, the updating of the base glance images is the best practice for security and software update compliance of instances.

Infrastructure host security and patching

Security is a fundamental part of the OpenStack architecture and security also needs to be maintained in order to protect the various security zones of the stack. OpenStack is a complex platform comprising many different component parts that are actively and continually being developed by an open source community. On the surface, this can seem fundamentally insecure; however, OpenStack is not only being developed by thousands of individuals, it is also being tested and scrutinized by thousands of users and developers. These users and developers create a useful feedback loop to other developers and testers. This provides almost constant vigilance against sloppy and insecure code. However, as in commercial software, a few security issues have still been discovered in underlying tools that are used by the OpenStack platform. This is why, the OpenStack Foundation has created an OpenStack Security Team that publishes advisories about identified security issues, descriptions, and links to patches.

Patching OpenStack code

These patches are for vulnerabilities in the code for OpenStack. The current security advisory list is maintained at `https://security.openstack.org/ossalist.html`, where patches are also provided. These patches are mostly upgraded Python files that can simply replace the existing code file on the OpenStack control or compute servers. An example of a patch that includes replacement files for a bug discovered in the neutron can be seen at `https://review.openstack.org/#/c/299025/`. The OpenStack Vulnerability Management Team is responsible for the bug and fix process for security and OpenStack at `https://wiki.openstack.org/wiki/Vulnerability_Management`.

Patching the operating system

A much larger part of the platform is the underlying operating system and/or tools. Since OpenStack can support many different hypervisors and run on multiple platforms, we will concentrate our discussion on Linux.

The Linux distributions that are most commonly seen running OpenStack are represented in the following chart, taken at the most recent OpenStack Summit (`https://www.openstack.org/assets/survey/OpenStack-User-Survey-Nov17.pdf`):

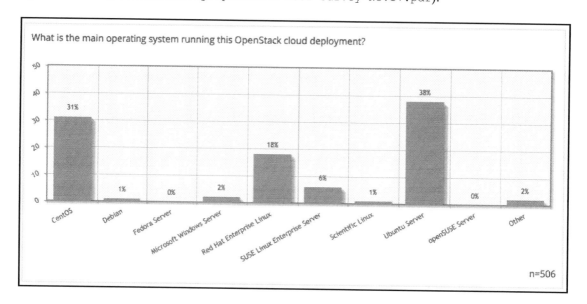

As the chart clearly shows, Ubuntu, CentOS, and Red Hat Enterprise Linux are the top three operating systems powering OpenStack today. Not surprisingly, two of these three distributions, Red Hat and Canonical (Ubuntu) are heavily involved with the OpenStack development community and the third distribution is not a commercial release, rather it is the Community Development Platform for the Red Hat family of Linux distributions (`https://wiki.centos.org/FAQ/General`). Therefore, CentOS is included with these, developing OpenStack to run on Red Hat distributions. CentOS typically releases bug fixes for OS issues within 72 hours of Red Hat delivering a new package.

Red Hat Enterprise Linux and CentOS

Using any distribution of Linux, it is vital to update any affected software in a timely manner to limit security risks. If the software is part of a package within Red Hat, the vulnerability should be patched as soon as it is released by Red Hat. Often, Red Hat includes patches with their security announcements and then releases it as a security erratum update. Again, it is vital to apply patches and updates as soon as they are released to help eliminate the risk of an attacker using the bug against your OpenStack infrastructure.

This can be accomplished using the Yum Package Manager to download from only trusted sources. These trusted sources could be the **Red Hat Network (RHN)** or a local repository that is under your organization's control. All downloaded packages from outside your organization should be verified for authenticity using the GNU Privacy Guard or GNUPG, a free package used for ensuring the authenticity of package files. If the verification fails, either the package is corrupt or it has been compromised.

Canonical Ubuntu-based operating systems

The Ubuntu security and patching ecosystem is very similar to Red Hat. Security updates are released by Canonical's Ubuntu developers whenever they discover and patch vulnerabilities. Security notices can be delivered via email or by subscribing through RSS. Ubuntu allows you to have security updates automatically installed—once configured, you won't need to run security updates manually again. However, best practice dictates that automatic patching only be used in lab and development environments. Ubuntu allows users to configure automatic security updates through unattended upgrades using `cron-apt`. Similar behavior can be applied to Red Hat hosts using `yum-cron` with `update_cmd = minimal- security-severity:Important`.

Software repository management

Software repository management is vital in order to provide secure updates to OpenStack infrastructure. Red Hat has developed a patch and upgrade management application named Satellite, and Canonical has named theirs' Landscape. Both of these are systems management applications that allow administrators to deploy, patch, manage, and monitor their respective systems. These applications are an on-premises way to download and manage content from remote software distribution portals. They reduce the amount of traffic over a corporate WAN during system updates as all packages are only transferred from the internet to the local repository once but served from the local repository many times. These applications also manage the update files locally to limit security risks of outside malicious content.

Satellite can even be configured as a single system or as a series of remote systems that act like proxies and are able to get authorization and subscription information from a central server. These commercial patch management applications also give users a single point of management for package management and allow the creation of individualized profiles to be created for separate classes of servers in the enterprise.

One alternative to using these vendor-specific tools is to create and maintain a package repository manually using open source tools, such as Puppet, Chef, and Ansible, by creating scripts that do replication and validation. However, a more complete option is to use a community project such as Pulp (http://www.pulpproject.org/). Pulp is a free and open source platform for managing software repositories. It is configurable to support RPM package types (rpm, srpm, errata, and so on), Puppet modules, Docker images, Atomic Trees, Python packages, and more. There is also a way to support Debian packages through a plugin. With Pulp, you can do the following:

- Pull in content from distribution repositories to the Pulp server manually on either a one-time-only or recurring basis
- Upload your own content to the Pulp server (OpenStack security patches)
- Publish content as a web-based repository, a series of ISOs, or various other methods

Software patching and repository management get incrementally more difficult as the number of hosts to be patched increases. Starting an OpenStack deployment with a proper patching strategy and the tools to manage and enable patching is critical for scaling and operating an OpenStack cloud. By applying and testing effective security patch strategies to the OpenStack infrastructure, first in lower environments and then in production, organizations will ensure that both the development and production environments are secure and tested for operations.

Hardening hypervisors

The Nova service, one of OpenStack's most complex projects, provides compute functionality in the environment. Nova is very pervasive throughout an OpenStack cloud and interacts with most of the other core IaaS services. Proper configuration of this particular service is an important factor in securing an OpenStack deployment.

Standard Linux hardening practices and hypervisors

The key to security in an OpenStack environment is the configuration and hardening of the virtualization technology, also named the hypervisor. Although OpenStack can be configured to use many different hypervisors, by far the most common hypervisor in use is KVM. All of the top operating systems, such as RHEL, Ubuntu, and CentOS, support the KVM hypervisor.

All of the top OpenStack distributions, such as Red Hat OpenStack Platform, Cisco, and SUSE, use KVM as the default hypervisor; other solutions like the one from Canonical have the ability to use LXC/LXD and KVM. Therefore, as KVM is a common default hypervisor for most OpenStack commercial platforms, we will focus our attention on the KVM hypervisor running on Linux for production grade security.

Additionally, the KVM hypervisor has been certified through the U.S. Government's Common Criteria program on commercial distributions and has been validated to separate the runtime environment of the instances from each other, providing adequate instance separation. For more information refer to `https://www.niap-ccevs.org/NIAP_Evolution/faqs/nstissp-11/`.

For example, on the Red Hat OpenStack Platform, one distribution that has been Common Criteria certified, had to satisfy the following list of minimal authentication requirements:

- Audit (ability to audit large amounts of events in detail)
- Discretionary access control
- Mandatory access control
- Role-based access control
- Object reuse (filesystem objects, memory, and IPC objects)
- Security management of administrative users
- Secure communication (SSH)
- Storage encryption (encrypted block device support)
- TSF protection (kernel software and data protection by hardware)

Although these identity and authentication functions are required for U.S. Government software certification, these are also best practice for production cloud environments, especially those operating in the public zone and connected to the internet. This guidance should also be combined into a larger logging, monitoring, and alerting framework that was discussed in `Chapter 5`, *Building to Operate*. Using similar tools to analyze workload logs such as ELK and other log processing and auditing tools will allow the ability for security alerts to be generated when any security events occur or alert thresholds are breached.

In addition to the basic identity and authentication requirements, as mentioned earlier in Common Criteria, many different cryptographic standards are available to OpenStack for identification, authentication, data transfer encryption, and protection of data at rest. Some of these are as follows:

- **AES**: Data in motion and data at rest
- **TDES**: Data in motion

- **RSA**: Data in motion and identification/authentication
- **DSA**: Data in motion and identification/authentication
- **Serpent**: Data at rest
- **Twofish**: Data at rest
- **SHA-1**: Data in motion and data at rest
- **SHA-2**: Data at rest and identification/authorization

It's not only the underlying operating system that must provide features to have optimal security, but the securing hardware that runs the compute host, and thus, the hypervisor should also support the following:

Feature	Hardware Description	Security Enhancement
VT-d / AMD-Vi	I/O MMU	PCI-Passthrough Protection
Intel TXT / SEM	Intel-Trusted Execution Technology	Dynamic attestation services
SR-IOV, MR-IOV, ATS	PCI-SIG I/O virtualization	Secure sharing of PCI Express devices by multiple instances
VT-C	Network Virtualization	Network I/O Improvements on hypervisors

In addition to hardware and operating system requirements, KVM also supports additional features, such as **SELinux and Virtualization (sVirt)**, Intel TXT, and AppArmor.

SELinux and AppArmor

At the heart of hypervisor security lies SELinux. SELinux is a labeling system where everything on the system receives a label that SELinux understands and can use for its policy sets. In most default configurations, it comes with multiple policy sets that define how processes with certain labels can interact with processes, files, directories, and so on, that have different labels. This access is enforced by the kernel and the configuration is extremely granular. Unfortunately, some find the configuration very challenging to understand and implement. However, most common adjustments are done through Booleans to toggle access on and off. For example, if a remote server wants to talk to SSHD locally, a single Boolean enables that access.

KVM provides excellent instance isolation through its standard use of MAC policies. This means that all instances run as processes, and they are confined using SELinux policies. In addition, KVM has an API for sVirt that ensures that all processes related to a specific instance can only access and manipulate files and devices that are related to that instance.

If an attacker were able to find a way to *break out* of the running instance, they would not get full interactive access to the underlying compute node's operating system. The attacker would instead be limited to only those files the instance had access to based on SELinux policies.

On the other hand, AppArmor does not use labels such as SElinux, but instead relies on a set of policy files that specify what to protect. This is accomplished by specifying a particular executable and what it is actually permitted to do. Policies are typically created for binaries such as `/usr/sbin/mysql` or `/sbin/dhclient` and have the ability to include different pluggable configurations for services such as `mysql` and `nameservice`. Capabilities are also configured in AppArmor to override certain default behaviors. However, the bulk of the policy will contain a list of files, directories, and so on and the behaviors that are permitted. For example, an AppArmor profile for MySQL would need to specify read access to the MySQL configuration files. This would be accomplished by adding the following to the policy file for MySQL:

- `/etc/mysql/conf.d/ r`
- `/etc/mysql/conf.d/* r`
- `/etc/mysql/*.cnf r`

These configuration parameters allow the MySQL binary to read the configuration files listed earlier. This behavior and configuration are very similar to Oracle's Trusted Solaris.

Systems running RHEL- and CentOS-based operating systems will see SELinux installed and in an `enforcing` state by default. AppArmor is included with most Debian-based systems including Ubuntu; however, the default behavior of enforcing or complaining varies by version. AppArmor can also be used with the LXD (Linux container) hypervisor that Canonical uses in its OpenStack platform distribution.

sVirt

sVirt is a solution that adds effective separation to virtualized environments using **Mandatory Access Control (MAC)** with implementations such as SELinux and AppArmor. This hardens systems against bugs in the hypervisor that could be used as an attack vector toward the hypervisor host or another instance running on the same hypervisor. SELinux uses a pluggable framework using MAC and allows guests and their resources to have unique labels. Once all of the instances, as well as the host, are labeled, rules can be created to allow or reject access across instances.

When using sVirt, the process works properly in the background, invisible to the instances themselves. Each instance's processes are labeled with a dynamically created label (500,000 are available), and these labels should extend to the actual disk images that belong to the instance's `qemu-kvm` process. Administrators are responsible for labeling the disk images. Once labeled, the instance no longer has any resources on the hypervisor that do not contain the label, and the instance will always start with this same label.

With SELinux set to enforcing on a system with a hypervisor, basic security is automatically extended to the instance to protect the host OS from the instance process; however, without an administrator adding the `system_u:object_r :virt_image_t` label to the images directory and the correct labels from the process to the individual instance image files, protection will be incomplete.

> Not all filesystems are compatible with SELinux labeling. For example, CephFS and not all NFS filesystems are not compatible.

SELinux and sVirt in action

The following instructions will allow you to check whether SELinux is enforcing (active and protecting). Since in your lab you're running CentOS 7, you should have SELinux installed and enforcing as well as all of the installed software to make sVirt work. We will show you how to set permissions on image files in order to protect your instances:

1. Execute the following commands as root on the lab server:

> Normally, in an HA environment, you would execute this command on a compute node.

```
# getenforce
Enforcing
```

Verify that the command responds with `Enforcing`.

2. If, for some reason, it is any other answer, do the following and repeat the preceding command:

```
# setenforce 1
```

3. Now, check your ID and your context:

```
# id
uid=0(root) gid=0(root) groups=0(root)
context=unconfined_u:unconfined_r:unconfined_t:s0- s0:c0.c1023
```

4. Now, let's find the context for the instance running on the lab server:

 You should have at least one instance running; if you have more than one, pick the first one. If you don't have any instances running, create an instance and repeat the command.

```
# ps axZ | grep qemu-kvm
system_u:system_r:svirt_tcg_t:s0:c55,c122 7480 ?
Rl    0:10 /usr/libexec/qemu-kv -name instance- 00000001
-S -machine pc-i440fx-rhel7.0.0,accel=tcg,usb=off
-m 512 -realtime mlock=off -smp 1,sockets=1,cores=1,threads=1 -uuid
b803b3ce-1570-
4092-8765-4a9f76793842 -smbios
type=1,manufacturer=Fedora Project,product=OpenStack
Nova,version=13.1.0- 1.el7,serial=8184f926-0263-4305-8d8d-
d50c1472697e,uuid=b803b3ce-1570-4092-8765-
4a9f76793842,family=Virtual Machine -no-user- config -nodefaults -
chardev socket,id=charmonitor,path=/var/lib/libvirt/ qemu/domain-
instance-00000001/monitor.sock, server,nowait -mon
chardev=charmonitor,id=monitor,mode=control -rtc base=utc -no-
shutdown -boot strict=on -device piix3-usb-
uhci,id=usb,bus=pci.0,addr=0x1.0x2 - drive
file=/var/lib/nova/instances/b803b3ce-1570-
4092-8765-4a9f76793842/disk,if=none,id=drive- virtio-
disk0,format=qcow2,cache=none -device virtio-blk-
pci,scsi=off,bus=pci.0,addr=0x4, drive=drive-virtio-
disk0,id=virtio-disk0, bootindex=1 -netdev tap,fd=26,id=hostnet0 -
device virtio-net-pci,netdev=hostnet0,id=net0,
mac=fa:16:3e:43:48:ad,bus=pci.0,addr=0x3 -chardev
file,id=charserial0,path=/var/lib/
nova/instances/b803b3ce-1570-4092-8765- 4a9f76793842/console.log -
device isa- serial,chardev=charserial0,id=serial0 -chardev
pty,id=charserial1 -device isa- serial,chardev=charserial1,
id=serial1 -device usb-tablet,id=input0 -vnc 0.0.0.0:0 -k en-us -
vga cirrus -device
virtio-balloon-pci,id=balloon0,bus=pci.0,addr=0x5
-msg timestamp=on
```

As you can see, the first line will give the context of `qemu-kvm` (instance process). The `instance-00000001` instance has an MCS context of `system_u:system_r:svirt_tcg_t:s0:c55,c122`.

5. Now, looking at the files associated with this instance in `/var/lib/nova/instances/b803b3ce-1570-4092-8765-4a9f76793842/` confirms that sVirt has properly labeled them the same as the instance processes (`s0:c55,c122`):

```
# ls -alZ /var/lib/nova/instances/b803b3ce-1570-
4092-8765-4a9f76793842/
drwxr-xr-x. nova nova system_u:object_r:nova_var_lib_t:s0 .
drwxr-xr-x. nova nova system_u:object_r:nova_var_lib_t:s0 ..
-rw-rw----. qemu qemu system_u:object_r:svirt_image_t:s0:c55,c122
console.log
-rw-r--r--. qemu qemu system_u:object_r:svirt_image_t:s0:c55,c122
disk
-rw-r--r--. nova nova system_u:object_r:nova_var_lib_t:s0 disk.info
-rw-r--r--. nova nova system_u:object_r:nova_var_lib_t:s0
libvirt.xml
```

If a virtual machine would happen to break out of sVirt confinement and was able to access objects on your lab server, it would only be able to use files in the same MCS context, which, in this case, is simply the image and console log, two files that are not extremely useful for compromising the host system.

If for some reason, SELinux is set to the **Permissive** or **Disabled** mode, all of this security is disabled. Ensure SELinux remains **Enforcing** in order to receive protection from sVirt.

As *cloud* has become such a hot topic, it only makes sense that cloud security has also been a very active topic lately. Keeping virtualized guests out of the host systems and out of each other's private files is critical in hypervisor security. Keeping virtualized hosts isolated to their own environments allows administrators to focus on hardening the host operating systems as well as enforcing security standards for guests instead of worrying about security breaches into the underlying infrastructure from their own workloads. This is another reason to keep the security *zones* for OpenStack management and instances separated. Limiting access to the OpenStack management zone is essential and most enterprises setup this zone as a non-routed network, not accessible from any external networks directly.

SSL and certificate management

Devices talking to one another securely without the possibility of data compromise is a constant goal for the security community. Considering some of the recent security discoveries, such as Heartbleed, BEAST, and CRIME, as well as the slew of new attacks discovered against government agencies, the need for cryptographic communications that can defeat eavesdropping attacks has increased exponentially.

At the beginning of this chapter, we defined security zones. These zones of networks and resources, along with a proper physical or logical network architecture, provide essential network and resource isolation of the different zones of an OpenStack cloud. For example, zones can be isolated with physical LAN or VLAN separation.

Assessing risk

With this best practice in mind, an administrator will first need to decide where the threat vectors are in their organization and where they are most vulnerable. One example would be the clouds that have public security zone services such as Horizon open to the Internet. As these endpoints are exposed to networks and users that are outside the organization's control, this endpoint is an obvious choice for high-security measures. However, securing the public endpoints may not be the only encryption needed on OpenStack endpoints. Depending on the organization's network architecture, threats could come from internal networks that may be connected to more secure OpenStack zones (management or private zones). As a result, it is insufficient to simply rely on OpenStack's default security zone separation in developing encryption security policy. Although adding encryption everywhere would certainly add an additional protection to all traffic, simply adding SSL/TLS encryption will provide no protection if an endpoint host is compromised. Therefore, endpoint encryption should simply be a part of a larger network and host-based security strategy.

Best practices for endpoint security

In today's standard OpenStack deployments, the default traffic over the public network is secured with SSL. Although this is a good first step, best security practices dictate that all internal traffic should be treated with the same secure practices. Furthermore, due to recent SSL vulnerabilities, SSL/TLS is the only recommended encryption method unless an organization absolutely needs legacy compatibility.

TLS secures endpoints with the **Public Key Infrastructure** (**PKI**) Framework. This framework is a set of processes that ensure messages are being sent securely based on verification of the identities of parties involved. PKI involves private and public keys that work in unison in order to create secure connections. These keys are certified by a **Certification Authority** (**CA**) and most companies issue their own for internal certificates. Public-facing endpoints must use well-known public certificate authorities in order to have the connections recognized as secure by most browsers. Therefore, with these certificates being stored in the individual hosts, host security is paramount in order to protect the private key files. If the private keys are compromised, then the security of any traffic using that key is also compromised.

Within the OpenStack ecosystem, support for TLS currently exists through libraries implemented using OpenSSL. We recommend using only TLS 1.2 as 1.1 and 1.0 are vulnerable to attack. SSL (v1-v3.0) should be avoided altogether due to many different public vulnerabilities (Heartbleed, POODLE, and so on). Most implementations today are actually TLS as TLS is the evolution of SSL. Many people refer to TLS 1.0 as SSL 3.1, but it is common to see the newest HTTPS implementations named as either SSL/TLS or TLS/SSL. We will be using the former in this document.

It is recommended that all API endpoints in all zones be configured to use SSL/TLS. However, in certain circumstances, performance can be impacted due to the processing needed to do the encryption. In use cases of high traffic, the encryption does use a significant amount of resources. In these cases, we recommend using hardware accelerators as possible options in order to offload the encryption from the hosts themselves.

The most common use case is to use SSL/TLS for OpenStack endpoints. Some solutions use an SSL/TLS proxy that can establish and terminate SSL/TLS sessions. While there are multiple options for this, such as Pound, Stud, nginx, HAproxy, or Apache httpd, it will be up to the administrator to choose the tool they would like to use.

Examples

The following examples will show how to install SSL/TLS for services' endpoints using Apache WSGI proxy configuration for Horizon and configuring native TLS support in Keystone. These examples assume that the administrator has already secured certificates from an internal CA source. If you will be publicly offering Horizon or Keystone, it is important to secure certificates from a global CA. These certificates should be recognized by all browsers, and they have the ability to be validated across the internet.

Let's start with Keystone.

Now that we have our certificates, let's put them in the right place and give them adequate permissions:

```
# chown keystone /etc/pki/tls/certs/keystone.crt
# chown keystone /etc/pki/tls/private/keystone.key
```

Now we can start the serious security work. We start by adding a new SSL endpoint for Keystone and then deleting the old one. First, find your current endpoints:

```
# keystone endpoint-list|grep 5000
```

Now create new endpoints:

```
# keystone endpoint-create --publicurl
https://openstack.example.com:5000/v3/ --internalurl
https://openstack.example.com:5000/v2.0 --adminurl
https://openstack.example.com:35357/v3/ --service keystone
```

Then, delete the old endpoints:

```
# keystone endpoint-delete <endpoint-id-from-above- endpoint-list>
```

Edit your /etc/keystone/keystone.conf file to contain these lines:

```
[ssl]
enable = True
certfile = /etc/pki/tls/certs/keystone.crt keyfile =
/etc/pki/tls/private/keystone.key
```

Now restart the Keystone service and ensure that there are no errors:

```
# service openstack-keystone restart
```

Change your environment variables in your keystonerc_admin or any other project environment files to contain the new endpoint by changing OS_AUTH_URL to the following:

```
OS_AUTH_URL=https://openstack.example.com:35357/v3/
#source keystonerc_<user>
export OS_CACERT=/path/to/certificates
```

Give it a quick test as follows:

```
keystone endpoint-list
```

Assuming that the command didn't display any errors, you can now configure the rest of your OpenStack services to connect to Keystone using SSL/TLS. The configurations are all very similar. Here is an example of Nova. You will need to edit the `/etc/nova/nova.conf` file to look like this:

```
[keystone_authtoken] auth_protocol = https auth_port = 35357
auth_host = openstack.example.com
auth_uri = https://openstack.example.com:5000/v3/ cafile = /path/to/ca.crt
```

Cinder, Glance, Neutron, Swift, Ceilometer, and so on are all the same. Here is a list of configuration files you will need to edit:

- `/etc/openstack-dashboard/local_settings` (Horizon access to Keystone)
- `/etc/ceilometer/ceilometer.conf`
- `/etc/glance/glance-api.conf`
- `/etc/neutron/neutron.conf`
- `/etc/neutron/api-paste.ini`
- `/etc/neutron/metadata_agent.ini`
- `/etc/glance/glance-registry.conf`
- `/etc/cinder/cinder.conf`
- `/etc/cinder/api-paste.ini`
- `/etc/swift/proxy-server.conf`

Once these or any other service configuration files have been modified, restart all of your services and test your cloud:

```
# openstack-service restart
# service httpd restart
# openstack-status
```

You should see all of your services running and online. You have now encrypted traffic between your OpenStack services and Keystone, a very important step in keeping your cloud secure. If not, check your services log files for errors.

Now we configure Horizon to encrypt connections with clients using SSL/TLS.

On the controller node, add the following (or modify the existing configuration to match) in `/etc/apache2/apache2.conf` on **Ubuntu** and `/etc/httpd/conf/httpd.conf` on **RHEL**:

```
<VirtualHost <ip address>:80> ServerName
   <site FQDN>
```

```
      RedirectPermanent / https://<site FQDN>/
   </VirtualHost>
   <VirtualHost <ip address>:443> ServerName
      <site FQDN> SSLEngine On
      SSLProtocol +TLSv1 +TLSv1.1 +TLSv1.2,
      SSLCipherSuite HIGH:!RC4:!MD5:!aNULL:!eNULL:!EXP:!LOW:!MEDIUM
      SSLCertificateFile     /path/<site FQDN>.crt
      SSLCACertificateFile   /path/<site FQDN>.crt
      SSLCertificateKeyFile /path/<site FQDN>.key
      WSGIScriptAlias / <WSGI script location>
      WSGIDaemonProcess horizon   user=<user> group=<group>
      processes=3  threads=10
      Alias /static <static files location>
      <Directory <WSGI dir>>
        # For http server 2.2 and earlier: Order allow,deny
        Allow from all
        # Or, in Apache http server 2.4 and later:
        # Require all granted
      </Directory>
   </VirtualHost>
```

On the compute servers, the default configuration of the libvirt daemon is to not allow remote access. However, live migrating an instance between OpenStack compute nodes requires remote libvirt daemon access between the compute nodes. Obviously, the unauthenticated remote access is not allowable in most cases; therefore, we can set up libvirtd TCP socket with SSL/TLS for the encryption and X.509 client certificates for authentication.

In order to allow remote access to libvirtd (assuming that you are using the KVM hypervisor), you will need to adjust some libvirtd configuration directives. By default, these directives are commented out but will need to be adjusted to the following in `etc/libvirt/libvirtd.conf`:

```
   listen_tls = 1
   listen_tcp = 0
   auth_tls = "none"
```

When setting the `auth_tls` directive to "none", the libvirt daemon is expecting X.509 certificates for authentication. Also, when using SSL/TLS, a non-default URI is required for live migration. This will need to be set in `/etc/nova/nova.conf`:

```
   live_migration_uri=qemu+tls://%s/system
```

For more information on generating certificates for libvirt, refer to the libvirt documentation at `http://libvirt.org/remote.html#Remote_certificates`.

It is also important to take other security measures in order to protect libvirt, such as restricting network access to your compute nodes to only other compute nodes on access ports for TLS. Also, by default, the `libvirt` daemon listens for connections on all interfaces. This should be restricted by editing the `listen_addr` directive in `/etc/libvirt/libvirtd.conf`:

```
listen_addr = <IP address or hostname>
```

In addition, `live_migration` uses a large amount of random ports to do live migrations. However, after the initial request is established through SSL/TLS on the daemon port, these random ports do not continue to use SSL/TLS. However, it is possible to tunnel this additional traffic over the regular `libvirtd` daemon port. This is accomplished by modifying some additional directives in the `/etc/nova/nova.conf` configuration file:

```
live_migration_flag=VIR_MIGRATE_UNDEFINE_SOURCE, VIR_MIGRATE_PEER2PEER,
VIR_MIGRATE_TUNNELLED
```

> The tunneling of migration traffic across the libvirt daemon port does not apply to block migration. Block migration is still only available by random ports.

Auditing OpenStack

As more enterprises are bringing production workloads to OpenStack, the need for audit compliance increases exponentially. These same enterprises may have specialized audit requirements for compliance with PCI, FEDRAMP, SOX, and HIPPA and without a way to audit what is happening in their cloud they are out of compliance. These enterprises are used to having this capability in legacy platforms; therefore, it only makes sense that they should require it with OpenStack.

This auditing needs to be done in a manner that the enterprises are accustomed to, and they should not be expected to have to ingest different log formats from each of the core OpenStack projects in a disparate fashion as they sometimes have to do today. However, the good news is that there is one format that provides a normalized and federated way to collect and analyze audit data. This format is the **Cloud Auditing Data Federation (CADF)** standard. The CADF standard defines a full event model anyone can use to fill in the essential data needed to certify, self-manage, and self-audit application security in cloud environments. This functionality is needed to build trust for the cloud platform and increase adoption. Enterprises need to feel that they are able to track and detect unauthorized access on their cloud platform.

CADF details

You can refer to the overview section at `http://docplayer.net/2573351-Cloud-audit-data-federation-openstack-profile-cadf-openstack.html` to understand what the CADF standard does—the Distributed Management Task Force, the governing body of CADF.

The CADF specification contains an event model that specifies taxonomies for any event that can be audited, these are as follows:

- **Resource**: The classification of the event by logical resource that is related to the event. Basically, this is who was the intended target or what observed the event.
- **Action**: This is used to classify what action caused the event.
- **Outcome**: This describes what the outcome of the action was.

Furthermore, there are mandatory properties of the preceding taxonomies, and these further break down the event into the following five components:

Model Component	CADF Definition
OBSERVER	The RESOURCE that generates the CADF Event Record based on its observation (directly or indirectly) of the Actual Event.
INITIATOR	The RESOURCE that initiated, originated, or instigated the event's ACTION, according to the OBSERVER.
ACTION	The operation or activity the INITIATOR has performed, attempted to perform or has pending against the event's TARGET, according to the OBSERVER.
TARGET	The RESOURCE against which the ACTION of a CADF Event Record was performed, was attempted, or is pending, according to the OBSERVER. Note: a TARGET (in the CADF Event Model) can represent a plurality of target resources.
OUTCOME	The result or status of the ACTION against the TARGET, according to the OBSERVER.

Required CADF event model components – CADF-OpenStack

Using these properties, the CADF data model is designed to provide the *who, what, when, where, from where,* and *where to* of an activity. Most people in security have heard of the 5 Ws of audit and compliance; however, this model was designed for cloud environments and adds an additional two (from where and where to).

In order to further explain how CADF is used in audit, based on the 7 Ws, refer to the following chart:

"W" Component	CADF Mandatory Properties	CADF Optional Properties (where applicable)	Description
What	event.action event.outcome event.type	event.reason (e.g., severity, reason code, policy id)	"what" activity occurred; "what" was the result
When	event.eventTime	reporter.timestamp (detailed), for each reporter event.duration	"when" did it happen • Any granularity via ISO 8601 format
Who	initiator.id initiator.type	initiator.id (id, name): (basic) initiator.credential (token): (detailed) initiator.credential.assertions (precise)	"who" (person or service) initiated the action
FromWhere		initiator.addresses (basic) initiator.host (agents, platforms, ...) (detailed) Initiator.geolocation (precise)	FromWhere provides information describ ing where the action was initiated from. May include • logical/physical addresses • ISO-6709-2008, precise geolocations
OnWhat	target.id target.type		"onWhat" resource did the activity target
Where	observer.id observer.type	reporterstep.role (detailed) reporterstep.reporterTime (detailed)	"where" did the activity get observed (reported), or modified in some way.
ToWhere		target.addresses (basic) target.host (agents, platforms, ...) (detailed) target.geolocation (precise)	ToWhere provides information describing where the target resource that is affected by the action is located. For example, this can be as simple as an IP address or server name.

CADF – the 7 Ws of audit – CADF OpenStack

To see more about the CADF profile for OpenStack, go to
https://www.dmtf.org/sites/default/files/standards/documents/DSP2038_1.0.0.pdf.

Using CADF with OpenStack

Except for a few special cases, getting CADF information out of OpenStack services is pretty straightforward. However, depending on the distribution, these instructions may differ.

The following instructions show how Nova can be enabled for CADF audit events to be sent to Ceilometer (optionally log files). This is done through the Keystone middleware, which provides an optional WSGI middleware filter that allows the ability to audit API requests for each component of OpenStack.

First, log in to your OpenStack deployment. Edit the /etc/nova/api-paste.ini file. At the end of the file, add the following code:

```
[filter:audit]
paste.filter_factory = pycadf.middleware.audit:AuditMiddleware.factory
audit_map_file = /etc/nova/api_audit_map.conf
```

Review the [composite:openstack_compute_api_v2] settings and verify that the values match the following sample:

```
[composite:openstack_compute_api_v2]
use = call:nova.api.auth:pipeline_factory noauth = faultwrap sizelimit
noauth ratelimit osapi_compute_app_v2
keystone = faultwrap sizelimit authtoken keystonecontext ratelimit audit
osapi_compute_app_v2 keystone_nolimit = faultwrap sizelimit authtoken
keystonecontext audit osapi_compute_app_v2
```

Additional options are available to redirect the events to log files as well as messaging. Simply, add the following code:

```
[audit_middleware_notifications]
driver = log
```

Now, copy the api_audit_map.conf file to the /etc/nova/ directory and restart the API service.

The command to restart the API service is OS specific. On Red Hat Enterprise Linux systems, the command is service openstack-nova-api restart. To find out more, refer to https://goo.gl/bNtm3K.

Open the entry_points.txt file in the egg-info subdirectory of your OpenStack installation directory.

For PackStack installations, the file path looks similar to `/usr/lib/python2.7/site-packages/ceilometer-2014.2-py2.7. egg-info/entry_points.txt`.

Although this example was only for Nova, there are preconfigured `api_audit_map.conf` files for other services, such as Glance, Ceilometer, Cinder, and Neutron at `https://github.com/openstack/pycadf/tree/master/etc/pycadf`. By following the preceding steps and using these `api_audit_map.conf` files, you can enable all core OpenStack services for CADF eventing.

Since the events are stored to messaging, and events, by default are sent to Ceilometer, this is where you will find your events stored. In order to query Ceilometer for Keystone events, you should first execute a Keystone action that would cause an event, as follows:

```
$ openstack user create test_user --os-identity-api- version 3 --os-auth-
url http://10.0.2.15:5000/v3 --os- default-domain default
```

In order to get the event that this created out of Ceilometer, you should do the following:

```
$ ceilometer event-list --query event_type=identity.user.created
```

It will result in the following type of output:

```
+------------------------+--------------------------------------------
------------------------------------------+
| Event Type | Traits
|
+------------------------+--------------------------------------------
------------------------------------------+
| identity.user.created | +--------------+--------+--------------------
------------------------------------+ |
|        | |    name   |     type      |
value | |
|        | +--------------+--------+---------
------------------------------------------+|
|        | | initiator_id  | string   |
asd123j123312yf34212339e6e424a7f         | |
|        | |   project_id  | string   |
ae7e3k14k202042j22f19bc25c8c09f0         | |
|        | | resource_id   | string   |
22a21766c478927349e3fda7ee0b712b         | |
|        | |   service     | string   |
```

```
identity.openstack.example.com        |  |
|     | +-------------+-------+---------
-----------------------------------------------+ |
+----------------------+-------------------------------------
-------------------------------------+ |
```

As we can see in the preceding output, we have an audit trail of who created the user from the preceding command as well as what the project was and the resource ID. This data and all of the data from the other services combined would provide a 7 Ws' audit trail for this user's transactions as well as any other transactions in this cloud. Using either open source tools, such as Ansible, Puppet, or Chef, to create query automation for Ceilometer, log files, or having Ceilometer feed this event data to something like IBM's QRadar http://www-03.ibm.com/software/products/en/qradar, which is, according to IBM:

"[A] security intelligence platform that combines traditional security information and event management (SIEM) and log management capabilities with network behavior anomaly detection (NBAD), vulnerability assessment and management, risk analysis and simulation and forensic data inspection. It consumes events, flows, asset and vulnerability information and network topology by integrating with other products/applications/services/assets/endpoints in a client's environment (on-premises or in the cloud), enabling users to view, analyze, understand and report on everything going on in their environment from many different angles and perspectives."

QRadar integrates with OpenStack as a consumer of Ceilometer data. It then takes the CADF-formatted data in the platform to do the analysis.

Log aggregation and analysis

As we saw in the previous section, we have an audit trail of who created the user from the demonstrated command as well as what the project was and the resource ID. This data and all of the data from the other services combined will provide a 7 Ws' audit trail for this user's transactions as well as any other transactions in this cloud. However, because we now have audit data, we can start looking for security attacks. Some of these attacks may be as follows:

- Real-time security alerts for brute force attacks an OpenStack
- Detecting malicious or unauthorized access to virtual machines, volumes, or images
- Accidental or intentional cloud service outages
- Compliance reporting for all user activity in OpenStack

These types of attacks can all be detected through log introspection. As we discussed in Chapter 5, *Building to Operate*, there is a set of OpenStack tools that have been the de facto standard for log shipping, formatting, and introspection. The three tools that make up this powerful combination are ElasticSearch (the searching module), LogStash (the log shipping tool), and Kibana (the visualization engine and dashboard). Although we discussed these tools mostly from an operational viewpoint in Chapter 5, *Building to Operate*, these same tools can be used to detect, in real time, all of the attacks listed earlier. The main advantages of this stack are as follows:

- Open Source search server written in Java
- Used to index many types of heterogeneous data
- Real-time search through indexing
- REST API web interface that outputs JSON

A best architectural practice in this area would be to use LogStash in a distributed fashion to centralize all log files with CADF data to a secure host running tools such as ElasticSearch and Kibana. LogStash could then be configured to index the highly normalized CADF logs, and limits would be created to alert on threshold breaches.

For example, if the CADF logs detected thousands of failed Keystone authentication events from the same IP address within a short time period. Chances are, this would be an indication of a brute force attack and would warrant an alert to the security and network teams.

Using a tool like Kibana, the teams can search through the audit logs and determine how long the attacks have been occurring, if anyone valid is logging in through the same subnet or any number of other analytics.

There are quite a few other SIEM platforms that do OpenStack integrations and can ingest either log files or Ceilometer feeds, some are listed here:

- Symantec Security Information Manager Splunk
- HP/Arcsight
- Tripwire
- NetIQ
- Quest Software
- Enterprise Security Manager
- Loom Systems (Sophie)

While both the open source and commercial solutions have great sets of features, it is up to each individual enterprise to evaluate SIEM solutions. However, with the preceding information, an administrator can feel empowered to enable CADF event logging for OpenStack and provide any platform with the data it needs to satisfy corporate audit requirements.

Summary

In this chapter, you learned some holistic approaches to OpenStack security. This includes not only the applications running on top of OpenStack but the projects that make up the platform as well as the underlying operating environments. You learned that enterprise OpenStack security is not only encryption, logging, or patching but a much more enterprise-based approach in which all solutions must work in harmony with others. Sometimes, this interoperability can be achieved with configurations; other times, it calls for additional open source or commercial grade enterprise software depending on security requirements. However, a very important point is to realize that OpenStack is no more insecure than its competing platforms and that there are strategies and tools available to make OpenStack compliant with most enterprise security policies.

Further reading

Please see the following for further reading relating to this chapter:

- https://security.openstack.org/ossalist.html
- https://review.openstack.org/#/c/299025/
- https://wiki.openstack.org/wiki/Vulnerability_Management
- https://www.openstack.org/assets/survey/April-2016-User-Survey-Report.pdf
- http://www.pulpproject.org/
- http://libvirt.org/remote.html#Remote_certificates
- http://www-03.ibm.com/software/products/en/qradar
- https://github.com/openstack/pycadf/tree/master/etc/pycadf

8
OpenStack Use Cases

As OpenStack continues to mature, so do the cloud installations of enterprises that have committed to the technology. Because OpenStack is a truly open platform, its use cases are only limited to the imaginations of those who decide to make it their cloud operating system. However, there are a few OpenStack use cases that have emerged as leaders in the enterprise adoption. These prominent use cases include web scale clouds improving DevOps functions, Big Data, Storage, NFV, and simple IT-as-a-Service. In this chapter, we will discuss some of these use cases and what makes them different from basic IaaS or PaaS implementations.

In this chapter, we will cover:

- Network Function Virtualization / Telco Cloud
- Big data and scientific compute use case
- Edge Computing use case

Network Function Virtualization (NFV) / Telco Cloud

To date, there has not been a single *killer use case* identified for OpenStack clouds. However, in the service provider industry, namely communication service providers, OpenStack has clearly been a major disruptor. In a survey conducted by Heavy Reading in 2016, it was reported that 86% of global telecommunication providers consider OpenStack essential or important to their business. Furthermore, the survey showed that telcos were accelerating adoption of NFV to increase business flexibility and speed as well as reducing costs while using OpenStack as the NFV IaaS platform. Almost 2 years later, we are seeing major telecommunication and service providers, such as AT&T, Deutsche Telekom, China Mobile, Reliance, and Verizon, all using NFV as the infrastructure of choice in production.

What is NFV?

The OpenStack Foundation describes NFV as *simply a new way to define, create, and manage network functions and services by replacing dedicated physical devices with software that can be automated and managed by OpenStack.* Just like virtual machines took the place of many dedicated servers in the data center, NFV simply continues the mindset of replacing proprietary and inflexible physical hardware with software. This is where a **Virtual Network Functions** (**VNF**) come in to play. VNFs are responsible for completing specific network tasks, and they can be VMs, a container, span multiple containers, multiple VMs, or bare metal servers all atop of the underlying compute and network infrastructure. VNFs vary in function as much as the physical devices that make up the telco services. Some examples of VNFs are mobile gateways, routers, content delivery network services, firewalls, WAN accelerators, DNS, and even packet core functions:

Proprietary physical infrastructure versus Network Virtualization Approach (Source: ETSI)

In general, most NFV benefits are centered around agility, flexibility, and simplicity. Today the telco industry is more competitive than ever and with margins decreasing, costs and the demand for new services increasing, NFV promises to deliver some new viable solutions. Some of the detailed benefits of NFV are as follows:

- Network flexibility through automated provisioning
- Taking advantage of open source technology and innovation
- The flexibility of drivers and plugins
- Full API accessibility and usability that enables faster development
- The use of COTS hardware versus proprietary appliances
- Operational efficiency from better orchestration across data centers, regions, and enterprises
- Complete troubleshooting transparency and documentation

The benefits of NFV on OpenStack (versus other platforms) increases efficiency as well as reduces Capex, Opex, power, and space requirements.

The difference between NFV and Software-Defined Networking (SDN)

Comparing SDN and NFV

Although NFV and SDN are similar, they are both distinctly different things. Both SDN and NFV are a way to provide virtualized functions and automation to network-related legacy networks, but the goal of SDN is different from NFV. SDN, which typically consists of a number of virtualized network items such as switching, firewalls, and routing are typically deployed on top of the physical network infrastructure that a cloud runs upon, often in an overlay network. These virtualized network services are typically part of the automation to deliver virtualized networks to instances using open source management tools that are specific and separate from NFV management tools.

NFV consumes these SDNs as part of a larger solution and then adds additional functionality on-top of SDNs. Some examples of this are virtual firewalls, content filters, antivirus applications, load balancers, routers, and so on. These additional functions are named VNFs or Virtual Network Functions. Although SDN plays an important role in the provisioning of NFV resources, the mission of NFV is to virtualize higher level network application functions on-top of SDNs in most cases.

NFV architecture

In recent years, NFV architecture has grown beyond simply being a proof of concept to the premier **Virtual Infrastructure Manager** (**VIM**) used to orchestrate automated service orchestration and management tools for NFV infrastructure. However, to better define the specifications of what an NFV platform should be, groups of OpenStack experts and telco industry leaders have created specific governance around NFV in Telecommunications.

European Telecommunication Standards Institute (ETSI)

Founded in 2012 by seven of the largest telco network operators, ETSI created the de facto Industry Specification Group for NFV. Within 5 years and over 100 publications later, what began as a proof of concept has now become the basis for interoperability testing. The results of this testing produce standards for member organizations and the European ICT industry as a whole.

ETSI is currently working on defining the architecture and requirements for VNFs to:

- Maximize stability and ensure service reliability
- Smooth integration with existing platforms and legacy EMS, NMS, OSS, BSS, and network orchestration services
- Develop highly performant and portable solutions that have wide application for service providers
- Maximize efficiency in migration to new virtualized platforms
- Simplify and streamline telco operations

Since 2012, there have been a lot of changes to the way the NFV ISG has been organized. To read more about the governance and hierarchy of the ETSI ISG see http://www.etsi.org/technologies-clusters/technologies/nfv.

Open Platform for NFV (OPNFV)

OPNFV is a Linux Foundation-hosted group that facilitates the development and evolution of NFV components across many different open source platforms and projects. Launched 2 years after ETSI, OPNFV assists in testing, deployment, and NFV reference architectures to accelerate adoption of open NFV platforms by enterprises. OPNFV develops reference architectures that ensure users that industry standards have been met while giving them architectures that offer componentized choices. Initially, OPNFV focused solely on the NFV infrastructure portion of the reference architecture (NFVI) which was based on the ETSI framework developed by the NFV ISG. Now this NFVI architecture comprises the virtualized infrastructure and the VNF managers, which instantiate the VNFs. OPNFV and ETSI share many of the same members that enable easier collaboration to help bolster specification activities. Both groups share a common mission, to stimulate an ecosystem that boosts NFV adoption. In 2018, ETSI and OPNVF are now closely collaborating by hosting *Plugtests* events to jointly test interoperability in France.

OpenStack's role in NFV

OpenStack and the ETSI NFV Architecture Framework (ETSI)

What is OpenStack's role in all of these NFV reference architectures? The preceding image is the basis for building all NFV systems. The reference architecture on the left shows the overall NFV architecture and the major components. The diagram on the right shows how different components of this NFV architecture work together. OpenStack's role is of the VIM. The VIM orchestrates the hardware contained in the **NFV Infrastructure (NFVI)** box to run VNFs.

Top requirements from Telcos for NFV on OpenStack

As we mentioned earlier in ETSI NFV and OPNFV, OpenStack is the fundamental choice for a virtualized infrastructure manager. The primary projects that are involved in the management of NFV infrastructure are Nova, Cinder, and Neutron. Other projects such as Magnum and Ironic can be involved in provisioning containers or bare metal servers for specialized VNF services. Although there are so many NFV enhancing features that have been enabled in OpenStack over the years, there are still some primary requirements for carrier grade usability for any virtualized infrastructure management platform. These are broken down into three main categories—performance, scalability, and high availability.

Performance

As you can imagine, with any telco-based cloud, network performance is paramount, specifically high-performance packet processing in and out of a VM to the larger network. One of the ways this can be accomplished is to give the VM direct access to the network through SR-IOV. In addition, Intel's DPDK-Accelerated Open vSwitch enables superfast packet processing and a multiqueue vhost-user with accelerated virtual switches. Both SR-IOV and DPDK are supported in OpenStack Neutron, and they are being used successfully by multiple large telcos. Similarly, having the ability to specify vCPU topology across cores, pin vCPUs to NUMA boundaries, and enable huge pages are also available in Nova. For more information on these optimizations,
see `https://wiki.openstack.org/wiki/VirtDriverGuestCPUMemoryPlacement`.

High availability, resiliency, and scaling

Most telecoms demand extremely high availability and reliability in their carrier grade infrastructure. Like most cloud platforms and native cloud applications, this is achieved by massive horizontal scaling. Although this may be a new convention for telcos because they have relied on an appliance and vertical scaling model, it will ultimately deliver telecoms additional reliability because it pushes more of the responsibility for availability requirements up to the application layer. Individual compute hardware in a cloud environment cannot provide 99.999% of uptime; however, applications running on many of these cloud hosts can provide it. With the distributed nature of cloud-based applications, the infrastructure monitoring can focus on increasing resiliency, monitoring, and failure detection. Beyond the distribution of OpenStack across a larger enterprise using a more cellular structure (using Nova cells), there are additional ways that are built into OpenStack that help increase availability and resiliency:

- VPN as-a-service drivers now work with HA routers
- Router HA using Neutron and L3 HA/VRRP when l2pop is enabled
- OVS agents can be restarted without affecting the data plane's availability
- VRRP networks can be configured to be separate from other traffic by network segmentation or physical network tagging
- Tools such as Monasca (Monitoring-as-a-Service) can process hundreds of thousands of metrics per second while scaling to service provider levels

Handling the rest of NFV management with NFVO and VNFM

NFVO or NFV Orchestrator is the function for onboarding new network services and virtual network function solutions, life cycle management, resource management, as well as validation and authorization of NFV infrastructure requests. The VNFM or VNF Manager is the overlord of the VNF instances. It handles the coordination of configuration and event reporting between the NFVI and the E/NMS or element or network management system.

The OpenStack Tacker project was created to take on both of these efforts. Tacker is based on the ETSI MANO Architectural Framework (see the previously mentioned image) and provides a functional stack of tools to orchestrate network services end to end using virtual network functions:

Tacker Architecture diagram

The functions that the Tacker project can accomplish are:

- **VNFM**:
  - Basic life cycle of VNF (create/update/delete)
  - **Enhanced Platform-Aware** (**EPA**) placement of high-performance NFV workloads
  - Health monitoring of deployed VNFs
  - Auto-healing / Auto-scaling VNFs based on policy
  - Facilitate the initial configuration of VNF

- **NFVO**:
  - Templatized end-to-end network service deployment using decomposed VNFs
  - VNF placement policy—ensure efficient placement of VNFs
  - VNFs connected using SFC—described in a VNF forwarding graph descriptor
  - VIM resource checks and resource allocation
  - Ability to orchestrate VNFs across multiple VIMs and multiple sites (POPs)

The NFV use case is solid and growing

By all indications, many telcos across many different countries have decided that OpenStack is the platform of choice for implementing NFV infrastructure. Contributions back to the OpenStack project from companies such as Verizon, AT&T, T-Mobile, China Mobile, NTT, and SK Telecom have shown that the NFV use case is growing at a rapid rate for OpenStack. Although many companies have developed a production solution for their NFV needs, many more are in other phases of implementation. Tools such as Tacker and other projects for NFV continue to grow and enjoy further adoption. The NFV use case looks like it will be a winner for many years to come.

Big data and scientific compute use case

When we think of large clouds of compute, storage, and network, many think of parallel processing, large amounts of data, and data analytics. However, in order to get to that panacea of cloud computing, we have to first design and orchestrate a solution. With data being generated from almost every device and being delivered through the network, it's very difficult to collect and store this data and almost impossible to perform analytics with traditional tooling. There are many approaches to solving this issue. Some of these are:

- **Hadoop**: Based on a filesystem called **Hadoop Distributed File System (HDFS)** and related technologies such as Map/Reduce
- **NoSQL**: MongoDB, Cassandra, CouchDB, Couchbase, and so on
- **NewSQL**: InnoDB, Scalebase, and newer technologies such as NuoDB

Hadoop is the leader in the market right now, but all of the solutions mentioned previously are based on the CAP Theorem (Brewer's conjecture). Unlike RDBMS, which was the leading solution to a universal data platform until about 5 years ago, none of these products met the following business requirements:

- Archive data
- Work with a variety of ETL solutions
- Encrypt data for policy, compliance, and governance
- Perform real-time queries
- Enable nontechnical personnel to write meaningful queries
- Minimize data movement

For example, if you had a large amount of data stored a relational database environment and you're expecting the data to grow exponentially, you will quickly find that with exponential growth comes an exponential reduction in performance. Some companies would spend millions on custom hardware to provide monolithic and vertically scaled hardware-based solutions, but what if you wanted to do it in the most economically feasible way and use an open source, fully orchestrated, and horizontally scalable way? You'd use OpenStack of course!

Storing Data – Hadoop

So how? Well, remember Hadoop? Hadoop is an industry standard framework for storing and analyzing a large dataset with a fault-tolerant Hadoop-distributed filesystem and a MapReduce (MapR) implementation. In recent years, the term Hadoop has come to refer to the framework and ecosystem of projects, not just Hortonworks, HDFS, or MapReduce. In the example mentioned later, we will use HDFS and MapReduce as examples. However, there are many other open source options for Hadoop filesystems and data processing.

HDFS is a filesystem used to prevent data loss similar to the way RAID prevents it; however, HDFS is a bit different. HDFS by default stores three copies of each data block in the cluster on different nodes in the cluster. Any time a machine fails that has one of these blocks, another block is created on a separate machine in the cluster.

HDFS operates in a write-once-read-many pattern. The datasets that are used in the cluster are copied once from the source and distributed across a cluster of servers. Because most times, the whole dataset, or a majority of it is used, it is critical that the time to read the whole dataset is more critical than latency (delay from input into the system to the desired outcome) in reading just the first record.

This distributed nature plays perfectly into the OpenStack's horizontal scaling architecture and nonproprietary commodity hardware compatibility. Hadoop cluster power can be harnessed using inexpensive hardware and scaled horizontally just like any other OpenStack use case:

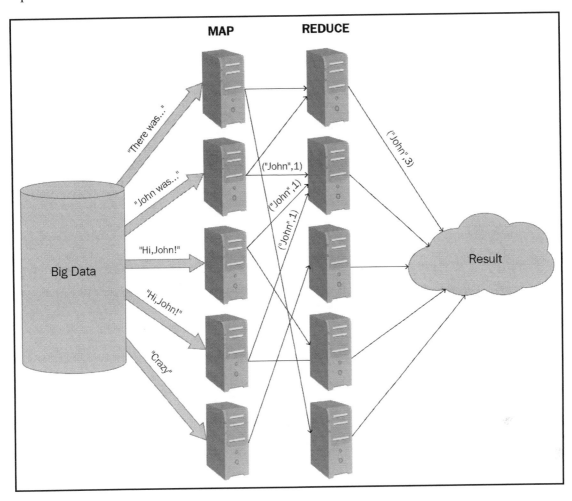

MapReduce Example (Source: http://dme.rwth-aachen.de/de/research/projects/mapreduce)

Combining Data - MapReduce

MapReduce is a model and opinionized implementation for analyzing and summarizing business and enterprise data using a distributed and massively parallel algorithm on a cluster of servers (such as HDFS clusters.) The *map* portion provides a programmatic way to filter and sort data, whereas the *reduce* performs the final summary operations. The model that ties MapReduce together also orchestrates the processing across the distributed servers. As HDFS clusters, this provides redundancy and fault tolerance to each task submitted and prevents data loss or extra delays based on execution stalls.

Hadoop-as-a-Service, OpenStack Sahara

The Sahara project was created to allow OpenStack users to have a simple and API-driven way to provision Hadoop, Spark, and Storm clusters by providing simple REST parameters and letting OpenStack take care of orchestrating the infrastructure. Sahara provides the means to scale clusters on demand by adding and removing worker nodes through API requests.

Some of Sahara's key features are:

- Fast provisioning of data processing clusters on OpenStack for development and **quality assurance (QA)**
- Using unused compute power from a general-purpose OpenStack IaaS cloud
- *Analytics as a Service* for ad hoc or bursty analytic workloads (similar to AWS EMR)

Key features are as follows:

- It is designed as an OpenStack component
- It is managed through a REST API with a **user interface (UI)** available as part of OpenStack Dashboard
- It provides support for a variety of data processing frameworks:
  - Multiple Hadoop vendor distributions
  - Apache Spark and Storm
  - Pluggable system of Hadoop installation engines
  - Integration with vendor-specific management tools, such as Apache Ambari, and Cloudera Management Console
- Predefined configuration templates with the ability to modify parameters

Example architecture for Hadoop Use Case

OpenStack Sahara Architecture (Source: https://docs.openstack.org)

The Sahara architecture consists of the following components:

- **Auth component**: This is responsible for client authentication and authorization; it communicates with the OpenStack Identity service (keystone).
- **DAL**: Data Access Layer, this persists internal models in DB.
- **Secure Storage Access Layer**: This persists the authentication data such as passwords and private keys in a secure storage.
- **Provisioning Engine**: This component is responsible for communication with the OpenStack Compute (nova), Orchestration (heat), Block Storage (cinder), Image (glance), and DNS (designate) services.

- **Vendor Plugins**: This pluggable mechanism is responsible for configuring and launching data processing frameworks on provisioned VMs. Existing management solutions such as Apache Ambari and Cloudera Management Console could be used for that purpose as well.
- **EDP: Elastic Data Processing**
  (EDP) https://docs.openstack.org/sahara/latest/user/edp.html is responsible for scheduling and managing data processing jobs on clusters provisioned by Sahara.
- **REST API**: This exposes Sahara functionality through REST HTTP interface.
- **Python Sahara Client**: Like other OpenStack components, Sahara has its own python client.
- **Sahara pages**: A GUI for the Sahara is located in the OpenStack Dashboard (horizon).

CERN – Big Data and OpenStack at Scale

The name CERN is derived from the acronym for the French *Conseil Européen pour la Recherche Nucléaire,* or European Council for Nuclear Research, a provisional body founded in 1952 with the mandate of establishing a world-class fundamental physics research organization in Europe. In the early days, CERN was mostly concerned with understanding the insides of an atom, the nucleus, and thus, the word Nucléaire.

Today, CERN's main charge is studying and researching particle physics, the study of the fundamentals of matter and forces that act upon it. Today, the labs at CERN are commonly referred to as the European Laboratory for Particle Physics.

Back in 2012, the CERN IT department decided to launch their very own private cloud based on OpenStack and other open source tools to gain efficiency and increase the speed at which they could provision infrastructure for researchers. Today, CERN's labs boast over 280,000 cores of OpenStack that are split into 60 different Nova cells.

Although CERN certainly has many different projects, which they are supporting with their cloud, the largest by far is for the data processing of the **Large Hadron Collider (LHC)**. With petabytes of data generated each time the LHC runs, plus over 200PB of historical data stored on tape, CERN needed to overcome a few problems with legacy ways of doing data analysis:

- **Latency variability**: Some results required files on disk and files on tape. How many files on tape affected how long the runs would take. This would cause latency variation.

- **Work distribution**: At times there would be a low number of files needing analysis and too many workers simply idling and vice versa. With a fixed number of workers available, it provided suboptimal performance and efficiency.
- **Failure intolerance**: Jobs fail, and when they do, the easier they are to troubleshoot and relaunch the better. CERN's legacy systems required constant operator intervention.
- Legacy home-grown analysis software written in C++.

CERN's solution to these problems was simply to use OpenStack, Sahara, and Hadoop (HDFS). With OpenStack and Sahara both being open source and written in Python, CERN's engineers had the ability to configure Sahara and OpenStack in a manner that solved any challenges they ran into and also allowed them to set up consistent data distributions and clusters in a repeatable and API-driven manner. CERN was also able to scale these clusters on demand. This was not possible with their legacy system.

Most recently, CERN has added OpenStack project Magnum to their stable of projects that allows them to provision Kubernetes, Docker Swarm, and Mesos clusters. They are testing these new platforms for additional ways to run data analysis.

Prior to the introduction of cloud Infrastructure as a Service, enterprises like CERN were forced to manually preprovision all their infrastructure based on use case and project-based requirements. Often, this would take weeks, if not months, to complete. Systems would be used during peak times and then sit idle or overprovisioned for large amounts of time. This idle capacity was then difficult to spin down and reconfigure for other projects. By adopting OpenStack, many enterprises that were doing big data analysis were now able to provision the infrastructure that was needed quickly and then when they were finished, just as quickly, they could return it to the pool of resources for other projects. It is no surprise that the big data use case is so popular for OpenStack adopters.

Edge Computing use case

For the past decade, we've seen a shift from decentralized customer-owned datacenter hardware and virtualization to centralized cloud models. Although this has generally been a boost to enterprises efficiency, time-to-market, and programmability, it has shifted the location-centric workloads of the previous decade back into a datacenter-centric model where network speeds and latency between customers and the datacenter satisfy most legacy workload needs. Almost as soon as cloud developers and architects began migrating workloads into the cloud, a new requirement emerged. This requirement was driven by IoT devices, sensors, smart cities, AR/VR, and even self-driving vehicles.

This requirement was in juxtaposition to the new datacenter-centric model that scaled regionally because some of the requirements were low-latency connections, resource-constrained locations, and possibly low bandwidth or unreliable networks.

Although OpenStack has grown to be a robust, stable, and flexible platform, it does have some expectations in regards to some of these new requirements, and it has become clear to the OpenStack Foundation that satisfying this new emerging use case is important. This particular use case has been called many names: distributed cloud, fog computing, far edge, and so on. However, the OpenStack Foundation is currently referring to it by a very simple name— Cloud Edge Computing.

What is Cloud Edge Computing?

Today's most mature definition of Edge Computing is the offering of cloud computing resources as well as an IT service environment at the network edge. This will bring compute, storage, and bandwidth much closer to the users and/or inputs of data. The applications that tend to require Edge Computing services are those that are sensitive to high-latency and unreliable connections and therefore cannot be serviced properly by centralized cloud resources in a distant data center. By moving some or all of the processing functions needed by edge applications closer to the end user or the input sources, Cloud Edge Computing can mitigate the latency and unreliability of widely distributed data center clouds.

Although Cloud Edge Computing sounds like something new, many of its requirements are the same as cloud computing:

- It can leverage commodity hardware
- It manages compute, storage, and network
- It uses and benefits from an open API to enable interoperability
- It benefits from the abstraction of many resource pools and uses virtualization
- It is multitenant and multiapplication capable

Here, Cloud Edge Computing differs from existing large datacenter-centric environments:

- Should be as close to users as possible thus improving user experience despite high-latency and unreliable connections.
- Services, location, and identity of the access links the edge site offers matters because many services have to be close to the right users and offer services to those particular users near the edge location.
- Edge sites can number in the hundreds to hundreds of thousands, and they are very dynamic. Specialized tooling for operations and governance must be developed for such a large landscape.
- Edge sites are mostly intended to be lights-out operations and may be remotely located with zero personnel.
- Edge locations may be resource constrained. Power, space, cooling, and network bandwidth all need to be considered at the edge when building and planning for expansion. Must be able to support all sizes of locations from data centers down to a single device.
- Security isolation is needed from national and regional datacenters to protect intrusions and attacks from spreading from edge nodes to larger sites.

As you can see, Edge Computing differs from centralized cloud computing by having the capability to support the needs of widely distributed sites, have potentially unreliable network connectivity and a high probability of having extreme challenges resources across sites within the scope of the total network. These particular challenges are typically not present in the centralized datacenter model and thus require different thinking in order to solve them.

Real-life use cases for Edge Computing

To better understand some of the many uses for Cloud Edge Computing, here are some possible use cases that have real-life impacts:

- **Autonomous vehicles and smart cities**: These applications collect telemetry data in real time. When IoT is used in vehicles and smart cities, they are extremely intolerant to high latency and require high bandwidth to satisfy the amount of streaming data being passed back to processing elements. Split second decisions are required and are made based on data being generated locally. Not only is this use case a demonstration of the need for extremely low latency but a need to do as much analysis and processing at an edge location in order to deliver near real-time data to the consumer.

- **Virtual reality and augmented reality**: Delivering high-bandwidth video and augmentation will require high bandwidth to the users and be very sensitive to network jitter. To stream data and video from national or regional datacenters to the immersive applications would be nearly impossible with today's technology. Therefore, in order to keep quality high, the edge would be tasked with responsibilities such as caching and optimizing content. Although content delivery networks are already used to solve a similar problem with online video delivery, VR/AR is a much more dynamic environment than simply making a static request for content and requires an environment that is able to process data as well as stream content and results.

- **Network Function Virtualization**: As more services are made available to customers from telco service providers, these services will take advantage of low-latency edge networks and edge infrastructure. Even today, in many edge sites, there are network appliances that are providing services that can be virtualized and put on edge infrastructure. Some existing business services such as managed router services, content filters, and caching could also be options hosting on the cloud edge sites.

- **Retail / Remote Corporate / Remote systems**: Edge systems could be created that work autonomously to host point of sale systems, manufacturing operations, or other vertical-specific applications. These edge systems could provide enterprises with fully autonomous infrastructure and be coupled into a distributed architecture to allow for more efficient operations. The distributed nodes could all be updated, patched, and modified as part of a larger automation platform. Furthermore, containerizing these workloads would begin to further push autonomous operation without regard for hardware differences. Cached content could provide relief from intermittent WAN outages, and the distributed nature of the applications would provide redundancy in the case of a regional or area-wide outage.

Current challenges with Cloud Edge Computing

Although some companies have already solved some of the issues with Edge Computing and are currently delivering solutions, as more use cases are developed, additional requirements will be discovered and push those in the Edge Computing community to think differently about solving these new challenges.

As mentioned earlier, Edge Computing has a set of different requirements that are unique from cloud computing. This creates some unique challenges that the OpenStack Foundation is looking to solve by creating a community around open Edge Computing. The largest of these needs is similar to the mano concept in NFV, an edge resource management system that can be a manager of edge sites in geo-distribution using WAN interconnects. This management system has to be designed to deal with network issues, bandwidth variation, and other IaaS issues and respond by making the needed changes to the distributed infrastructure to compensate. This system would also have to have the functionality to deal with the constraints of the differently sized edge nodes and their resource constraints.

Some of these issues can be addressed by modifying existing tools and projects within OpenStack stable; however, there are other more challenging aspects that will require further research and development as follows:

- Monitoring capacity across all edge nodes simultaneously.
- Physical security issues at edge sites, especially those that may be simply pole mounted or embedded in public access areas.

- For those sites without local storage or needing shared storage, managing WAN latency to data.
- Deploying capacity and additional edge sites, often remotely and without hands and eyes support.
- Orchestration of the workloads to be used at edge sites as well as balancing the distributed workload across multiple edge locations.
- Federating edge sites into larger clouds, thus setting up a cloud-of-clouds model. This type of model would simplify overall IaaS resource scheduling but introduces additional complexity.
- Some sort of network state service would have to be created to track overall health status from the core of the infrastructure to track overall state even with the lack of network link continuity.
- Application demand analysis across edge sites to track where applications are needed and at what levels.

Although this description of Edge Computing and its challenges is far from exhaustive, it is representative of some of the efforts that have been happening inside and outside of the OpenStack community. While OpenStack is not the only option in infrastructure management for Edge Computing, its flexible framework and open nature make it a logical and attractive choice. The OpenStack Foundation is asking the open source community to rally around these new ideas and challenges. They are hoping, just like with OpenStack, a community of the brightest engineers and architects in the world can solve some of these edge challenges and help create tools to meet the new requirements.

For further information and to get involved, see:

- **OSF Edge Computing web page** (https://www.openstack.org/edge-computing)—A central place to find pointers to videos of previous events, articles, and further content on edge computing.
- **OSF Edge Computing mailing list** (http://lists.openstack.org/cgi-bin/mailman/listinfo/edge-computing)—A forum for discussions concerning edge and Edge Computing (not exclusively OpenStack) and to receive information about ongoing activities and calls for action.

Summary

In this chapter, we looked at three major use cases for OpenStack. NFV, a use case that is in production in the majority of major Telcom enterprises worldwide. A big data use case that is being used by one of the largest and most significant particle physics laboratories in the world, and Edge Computing is an emerging use case that is quickly becoming one of the future focus areas of innovation in the OpenStack Foundation. There are many more use cases, and the examples of these use cases are located on the OpenStack Foundation website at `https://www.openstack.org/user-stories/`.

9
Containers

Container technology continues to be on the minds of most OpenStack and non-OpenStack users and operators. Among the current adopters of containers on OpenStack, 47% are also attempting container management using Kubernetes. In this chapter, we'll look at what container technology brings to OpenStack and how it is further evolving into the infrastructure of OpenStack itself:

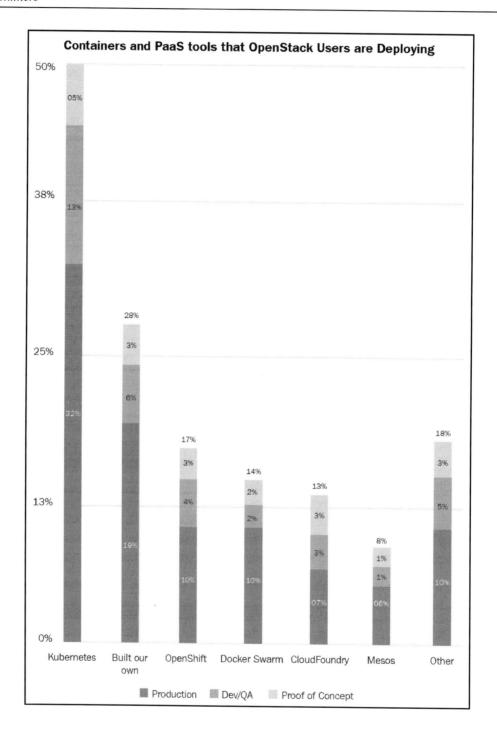

In this chapter, we will cover the following topics:

- Containers and OpenStack
- OpenStack container-related projects

What are containers?

Since the 1970's, there has been research on how to separate applications from the host systems that they run on. In 1979, Unix V7 introduced us to the `chroot` system call that isolated a `root` directory of a process and it's children to a separate location on the host's filesystem, thus protecting the underlying host from prying eyes or malicious intent. Since then, we've seen developments such as FreeBSD jails (2000), Linux vServers (2001), Sun Solaris Containers (2004), LXC (2008), Warden (2011), Google's *Let Me Contain That For You*, and Docker in 2013.

Although some of these technologies are still around, most of them were the basis for future developments in container technology. This technology allow developers to package an application with all the required libraries and dependencies it needs and ship it as one complete package. Much like many different manufactures do today with durable goods like furniture and other premanufactured and self-assembled goods.

In some ways, containers can act like virtual machines. Some containers, like LXC and Oracle Solaris bring more of the underlying operating system with them. In each case, containers, from the outside, look a lot like they have a complete operating system with them. However, unlike virtual machines, they aren't a copy of a full operating system. As stated earlier, they are simply a set of individual components that are needed to fully operate the selected application or workload of the container. This increases efficiency and performance of both the container and the underlying host by reducing the requirements for each application down to the bare essentials.

Because containers include everything the workload needs and nothing it doesn't, they are also much quicker to bring up and down. Unlike traditional virtualization that boots up whole operating systems that have to go through pre-boot and checks of virtualized hardware, containers skip these steps by relying on the host operating system to have the infrastructure and drivers ready. Having only what is needed from the operating system in a container also brings the added benefit of removing much of the operating system and reducing the attack surface of what's running. This increases security by limiting what can be exploited or compromised. Containers can also be further secured from their host using VM security technologies that were discussed in the Security chapter, so the compromise of the whole underlying host by breaking into a container is significantly reduced.

Of course, another reason to like many container technologies is that they are open source. This means that they have broad community support and a wide ecosystem of supported drivers, plugins, and other interoperability features. By being open source, container platforms have an organically grown contributor network that helps foster innovation and rapid development.

So why are people so excited about containers?

People have been excited about container technology for years, but most recently, the Docker open source project has captivated the attention of the developer community. Being flexible and building on the concept of easy deployment that was made popular by other open source software like Vagrant, Docker made it easy to explore the development of microservices with only a few command lines in a wide array of host operating systems.

These containers supporting microservices are designed to develop applications in which multiple complex operations are separated into smaller composable parts that, when assembled into a workflow, complete the same tasks as legacy monolithic applications. When each part is assembled separately and placed into a container such as Docker it can be scaled, upgraded, and monitored independently. This increases efficiency, reliability, and scalability.

How do I manage containers?

Just like OpenStack orchestrates VMs and workloads, tools are needed to orchestrate container technologies such as Docker. In order to bring these technologies together and enable scaling, enhanced reliability, and manageability in a consistent manner, a management tool must be used. One of the most popular tools for this purpose is called Kubernetes. Kubernetes is an open source tool used to manage containers and clusters of containers. It provides the tools for deploying, scaling, and managing changes to existing applications. It also helps you optimize the underlying resources that are supporting the containers on a system. It is extensible, and it provides fault-tolerance by providing a highly available architecture to applications.

Containers and OpenStack

Now that we know what containers are, we can discuss how they are beginning to impact OpenStack, both in terms of architecture and workloads. First, we will discuss how containers are perfect for being run on OpenStack and how they can be operated in the tenant space using new and existing projects. Second, we will cover how several OpenStack distributions are using container technology to drive additional efficiency, resiliency, and high availability into the OpenStack control plane.

Docker on OpenStack

Why would anyone want to run Docker on OpenStack? First, OpenStack has built-in drivers for launching docker containers with the same method as VMs, using Nova. This driver has been around a long time and works very well. There's a lot to be said for having a single orchestration platform for containers, VMs, and bare metal. Even without launching the direct virtualization driver for Nova to create native Docker containers, users can simply provision VMs with images that have been stripped down and are for hosting Docker containers. There's been a lot of talk about running containers on bare metal inside OpenStack using Ironic or outside of OpenStack on these purpose-built Linux distributions. This method of deploying containers is usually suggested as a way to gain further efficiencies since a hypervisor like KVM does consume some amount of resources beyond what a bare metal host would consume. It is true, running VM on top of a hypervisor such as KVM then using it as the Docker platform host does have a performance cost. However, in hallway discussions, this performance hit ranges anywhere from 5% to 20%, but in reality, on a properly tuned system, it is actually less than 5% in many performance measurements. One example, shown at `https://forum.level1techs.com/t/how-fast-is-kvm-host-vs-virtual-machine-performance/110192` demonstrates KVM CPU performance is only 4.5-5.1% different from bare metal using a windows image as an example. Another presentation by Wataru Takase shows real comparisons between KVM and host-based Docker instances on OpenStack at `https://www.slideshare.net/WilsonCunalata/docker-vs-kvm`. If you're looking for the absolute most efficiency, then Docker on the compute hosts, driven by Nova is the best choice. However, tenants are at the mercy of the OpenStack infrastructure administrators for configuration and versioning. Using Docker on VM, users have complete control of the environment that allows them to have a true multitenant environment to share networking and storage with other types of compute (VMs / bare metal / docker).

Kubernetes on OpenStack

One abstraction layer up from containers and OpenStack orchestration is Kubernetes. This deployment platform for containerized applications can be deployed on OpenStack to manage containers running on VMs in OpenStack, bare metal hosts, and host-based containers. It's perfect for the OpenStack platform because it lets operators not only manage deployments but manages application life cycle and scaling. It can also be used in combination with Keystone to provide role-based access control:

If you're looking to build an environment where it's an absolute fact that everything will be in containers and be orchestrated with tools like Kubernetes only, there's little benefit to running OpenStack for this type of environment. In this case, a full bare metal deployment may be the best choice. However, OpenStack, like other open infrastructure choices, provides a valuable feature—options and more options. If you're looking to architect a flexible solution that gives access to containers, container orchestration services, VMs, bare metal to other options like Mesos, and Docker Swarm clusters with shared networking and storage. Even more important, OpenStack is a platform that has shown extreme flexibility and an ability to morph into whatever technology is next.

OpenStack container-related projects

You learned in earlier chapters that OpenStack comprises composable services that, together, can deliver a unified infrastructure delivery system. This means that you can put together different combinations of services in an OpenStack cloud to meet different needs while having the core projects deliver the requisite services needed to operate an OpenStack cloud. When designing an OpenStack cloud for accommodating containerized applications there are quite a few options available. Let's look at some services that work in conjunction with others to provide container services.

Nova-Docker

Nova-Docker started as the project to bring Docker functionality to the compute project Nova. It was forked to its own project because the life cycle of VMs and Nova and Containers and Nova were quite different. The development of many other container-based projects led to the closure of the Nova-Docker project, but support in Nova remains for provisioning containers. Nova-Docker and the Nova driver set for containers was the start of full-fledged support for Docker. The alternative to Nova-Docker is Zun, which will be discussed in detail later in this chapter.

Integration with Neutron – Kuryr

Kuryr and Neutron provide advanced network functions to containerized workloads through libnetworks. This project's goal is to try and prevent the reinvention of networking for containers running on OpenStack. For example, the Magnum project uses its own networking and abstraction layer to provide network services to containers it orchestrates. Kuryr uses the current abstraction layer and hard work that was put into Neutron and provides production grade networking to containers. Kuryr aims to be the integration into Neutron for container services, not a separate networking service. Kuryr aims to be most effective in the area between Docker and Neutron to drive changes to both projects to fulfill the use cases needed to provide container networking.

It's important to note that Kuryr is not a networking solution on its own and that it acts as a *courier* between containers and Neutron networking. In short, Kuryr creates a relationship between Docker networks. For example, after installing Kuryr, you can create a test network for Docker by executing the following code:

```
$ docker network create --driver kuryr docker_network
hpxRK5usaatIeVvfH8C5ipDYr9Stfh4mwr34nlllkCToldtTbVOh8i6pfMHkRBvd
$ docker network ls
NETWORK ID          NAME                DRIVER
231f8c1b5ae4        docker_network      kuryr
```

Integration with Cinder – Fuxi

During the Mitaka release cycle, a project named Fuxi was created to give Cinder and Manilla volume access. This is needed to increase the performance of data writes and to give persistence to volumes that contain data that may be needed after a Docker container is terminated. Fuxi leverages the Docker API to create volumes that are backed by OpenStack Cinder or Manilla storage. These volumes can also be shared between Docker containers:

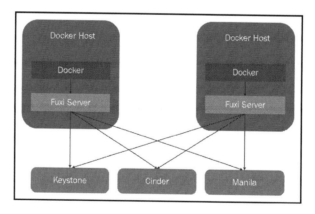

Fuxi Docker Architecture

Fuxi consists of a Fuxi server that runs on each of the Docker hosts, whether it is a Nova instance or a bare metal host. The Fuxi server then translates Docker calls for storage into Cinder and Manilla API calls.

Fuxi can be installed through `pip` and its use is straightforward. See the following example:

```
$ # Create cinder volume

$ docker volume create --driver fuxi --name my_vol \
    --opt size=1 \
    --opt fstype=ext4 \
    --opt multiattach=true \
    --opt volume_provider=cinder

$ # Reuse existing cinder volume
$ docker volume create --driver fuxi --name existing_vol \
    --opt size=1 \
    --opt volume_id=125da087-8b89-46de-97e4-c275c9a5bd1a \
    --opt volume_provider=cinder

$ # Create generic manila volume
$ docker volume create --driver fuxi --name my_vol \
    --opt volume_provider=manila

$ # Run container with volume
$ docker run -v my_vol:/var/www httpd
```

As you can see, operating Fuxi is as straightforward as creating a VM, it can be done through the Docker API or through the command line as shown previously.

Magnum

Magnum is an API-driven OpenStack service that makes container orchestration services such as Docker Swarm, Kubernetes, and Apache Mesos available like other services in OpenStack:

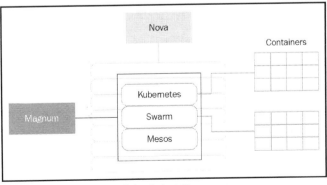

An introduction to Magnum

Magnum allows multiple container technologies to live together in harmony on a variety of Nova instance types, such as containers, bare metal, and VMs. Beyond Nova, Magnum provides container-specific features and subsequent API extensions. It provides these features in a way that is completely consistent with OpenStack and other services. It also allows the use of native clients such as the Docker CLI client, which eliminates the need to redesign the service each time the underlying tooling changes.

Containers created in Magnum are named *Bays*. These are collections of Nova instances that are normally created by Heat and orchestrated by Heat templates. Because Heat is coordinating the creation of these images through Nova, the target for these images can be VMs or bare metal. Other services such as block storage (Cinder) and database services (Trove) can be created by Magnum and placed into bays where they can create application containers:

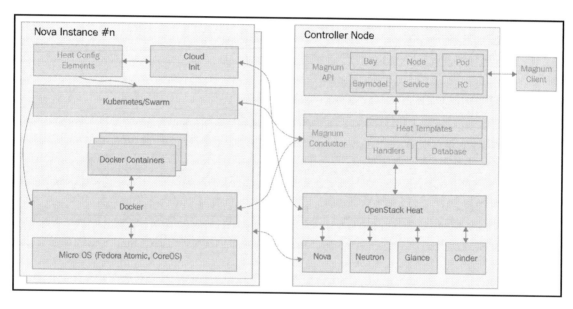

OpenStack Magnum Architecture (OpenStack Documentation)

Identity services are also integrated into OpenStack by leveraging Keystone. Networking services, as mentioned earlier in this chapter, are satisfied using the Flannel overlay network, which allows container management engines like Kubernetes to assign IP addresses to containers in each bay and allows multihost communication between containers. This is specific to Magnum and does not integrate with Kuryr. The Magnum and Kuryr groups are still working toward the integration of Magnum with libnetwork and Kuryr; however, this work is still in progress.

Magnum provides security to its workloads, bays, and instances by restricting access to them down to the tenant that created them. Bays cannot be shared between tenants and each bay cannot run on the same kernel as neighboring bays. This is important because it adds a layer of multitenancy to containers that container management applications like Kubernetes leaves up to the individual implementer. In short, this security model mimics the model used by Nova users when creating instances on the same compute node, but by different tenants.

Zun

If you're just looking to run containers in OpenStack and don't want a Kubernetes cluster deployed for you, then Zun is for you. Zun is for those who want to create containers and put workloads on them from, say, Docker Hub or some other repository without having to create pods or clusters as part of the exercise. OpenStack's solution for this is Zun, a container management service. Zun lets you run any container, and it will even let you provision bare metal through Ironic. Also, it will show up in Nova the same way any other instance would. You're probably thinking *it can't be this simple!* It is simple, as simple as the `zun create [Docker container name]` command. As you can see here, Zun has deep integration with the other core OpenStack projects:

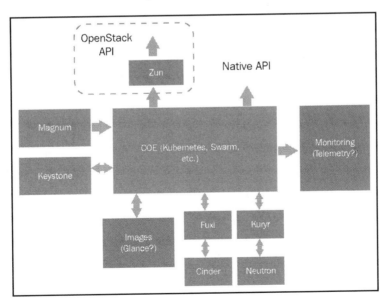

What is Zun? (https://bit.ly/2IHpDE2)

Some examples of how to create and run Docker containers in Zun are listed later in the text. Although all these functions are available through REST API, the following examples are based on the Zun command-line client (CLI):

First, find an image from an image store such as Glance or Docker Hub:

```
$ docker search cirros
```

Now run a container, start it, and let it execute a command, as follows:

```
$ zun run cirros ping -c 4 google.com
```

How about attaching to a running container:

```
$ zun attach [containername]
```

How about using Heat to launch Wordpress into containers:

```
resources:
 db:
   type: OS::Zun::Container
   properties:
     image: mysql
     environment:
       MYSQL_ROOT_PASSWORD: rootpass
       MYSQL_DATABASE: wordpress
wordpress:
  type: OS::Zun::Container
  properties:
    image: "wordpress:latest"
    environment:
      WORDPRESS_DB_HOST: {get_attr: [db, addresses, private, 0, addr]}
      WORDPRESS_DB_USER: root
      WORDPRESS_DB_PASSWORD: rootpass
```

As you can see, Zun is as useful as it is simple. Altough Nova-Docker may have been the originator of containers that leverage Nova, Zun is a fully featured service that is not limited by the Nova API as it provides its own API interface. Zun is a very simple container management tool inside of OpenStack that doesn't look to compete with Kubernetes and doesn't aim to. Zun leverages Heat for orchestration, looks to Magnum and Kargo to tackle COE provisioning, suggests Nova-lxd (system containers from the Nova API), and doesn't look to be the service that builds containers from source code (see Solum project).

Earlier, we've shown you a few ways that OpenStack can be integrated with container workloads. From setting up Hadoop clusters to simple one container microservices, containers can integrate with all of OpenStack's core services such as Keystone, Cinder, Neutron and Nova. Whether you want to run containers independently, on top of instances, or in bare metal through Ironic, you can do it with OpenStack.

OpenStack On Containers

We've talked about containers on OpenStack, but as OpenStack evolves, more motion is being directed to running OpenStack on containers. Today, the most common architecture for OpenStack clouds consists of one or more bare metal servers that house the control services in order to operate OpenStack. When configured for high availability, these bare metal servers can scale horizontally, but for the most part, they will contain the exact same control plane services on each server. We call this a monolithic control plane design. The limitations of this design are mostly centered around scaling the services, both stateful and stateless. Although most of OpenStack's stateless servers can scale horizontally very wide, there are some issues with the stateful services and the way they are load balanced. This presents limitations to horizontal scaling; for example, when scaling corosync, you are limited to 16 cluster members, in some cases more, but none have been well tested. Corosync is the open source program that works in conjunction with pacemaker to create the availability clusters within some distributions of OpenStack. Corosync is the daemon that provides cluster membership and messaging capabilities that are key to keeping stateful services like OpenStack's database in sync and highly available.

In addition to the high availability issues, if OpenStack is running on bare metal and those services are hard bound to the infrastructure underneath, even if they are in a HA configuration, all services will need to be disabled when upgrading both the operating system and the hardware or for other maintenance activities. This reduces the availability of the control plane by a significant percentage in most enterprises. In addition, when upgrading OpenStack, these services that are running on the bare metal hosts, must be shut down in order to upgrade. They don't possess immutable and scalable properties and are not managed like containers under Kubernetes.

In addition, if the workloads on OpenStack are migrating to cloud native microservices architectures, then it would make sense that the OpenStack control infrastructure should be moving in the same direction. Fortunately, most OpenStack distribution vendors have begun the process of moving to a completely disaggregated nonmonolithic model for future OpenStack architectures.

However, there are already many open source projects that have taken great strides to bring this type of containerized architecture to OpenStack. Below, we will discuss some of these projects.

Kolla

The Kolla project is described as a service that provides production-ready containers and deployment tools to operate OpenStack clouds that are scalable, fast, reliable, and upgradable using community best practices. In short, the Kolla project installs OpenStack into containers. However, there are two subprojects. One project, kolla-ansible uses the popular configuration management tool Ansible to create highly opinionated, yet, fully customizable OpenStack deployments fairly easily. There are plenty of options for more advanced users, but it does not install any sort of container management platform to manage the containers it deploys. Kolla-ansible instead relies on the pure functionality of Ansible for upgrading, scaling, and configuration operations.

Another option is kolla-kubernetes. This version of kolla deploys OpenStack on top of Kubernetes. This allows all the operational and managerial functions of Kubernetes to be applied to the containers running OpenStack services. This enables OpenStack to be deployed and run as a set of services that previously would have been stacked together in a single monolithic architecture. Now, running as services under Kubernetes, they can be spread across multiple bare metal hosts or VMs and the services themselves can scale horizontally without being bound by hardware or logical cluster restraints.

Unfortunately, kolla-kubernetes is still in its early stages and installing it is beyond the scope of this book. However, if you would like to try it, instructions can be found at `https://docs.openstack.org/kolla-kubernetes/latest/`.

Unfortunately, even with Kubernetes, there are still some challenges in running OpenStack on containers. Kubernetes lacks multitenancy, is not in a lot of production workloads, is not good at running VMs, and doesn't support complex networking technology. Kubernetes is also changing at a high velocity, not something most enterprises want supporting their production infrastructure. These are only some of the reasons Kubernetes hasn't quickly become the de facto container manager for OpenStack on containers. However, Kubernetes is making great strides and OpenStack managed by Kubernetes looks to be the direction the platform is heading.

Helm

Inside kolla-kubernetes is a very interesting project named OpenStack Helm. Helm, a project started by Google, and Deis is a Kubernetes package manager designed to manage the entire life cycle of an application that is running inside Kubernetes. Some of its features include application bundling, a robust template language and engine; it supports upgrade and rollback of services and improves overall CI/CD workflow. OpenStack Helm started in 2016 at AT&T as an internal project that became an official project in 2017. Helm helps you define, install, and upgrade both simple and complex Kubernetes applications using Helm charts. A Helm chart is a collection of files that describe a related set of Kubernetes resources. A single chart may be used to deploy a simple application or something more complex like a full web app stack. Charts are created as files laid out in a directory tree where they can later be packaged up into versioned archives and deployed. The following is an example of a Helm chart directory structure for a Wordpress application chart:

```
wordpress/
   Chart.yaml      # A YAML file containing information about the chart
   LICENSE         # OPTIONAL: A plain text file containing the license for
the chart
   README.md       # OPTIONAL: A human-readable README file
   requirements.yaml # OPTIONAL: A YAML file listing dependencies for the
chart
   values.yaml     # The default configuration values for this chart
   charts/         # A directory containing any charts upon which this chart
depends.
   templates/      # A directory of templates that, when combined with values,
              # will generate valid Kubernetes manifest files.
   templates/NOTES.txt # OPTIONAL: A plain text file containing short usage
notes
```

The OpenStack Helm project provides charts for 50+ OpenStack-related services. These are used in conjunction with Ansible and Kolla to deploy complete Kubernetes OpenStack deployments. For more information, see https://docs.openstack.org/openstack-helm/latest/readme.html.

Summary

In this chapter, we looked at some of the requirements driving container adoption on and under OpenStack. We looked at some of the most popular OpenStack projects that are driving further container adoption and interoperability of OpenStack with cloud native container applications. It is very important to remember that container adoption is driven by application availability and that adoption will happen over time. Therefore, just as we see many enterprises ready to take on a cloud first posture, we see the same enterprises still running legacy workloads on bare metal, in virtualized environments, in private clouds as VMs, and as containers in public clouds. Fortunately for these enterprises, bare metal, VMs, and containers can all be orchestrated with one tool, OpenStack. In the coming years, with continued container adoption and management platform development, infrastructure orchestration will continue to grow and develop, just as OpenStack did, and it will be critical as an architect to choose the right tool for the job.

10
Conclusion

Like all technology, OpenStack changes and evolves. Since we wrote the first edition of this book, OpenStack has evolved into a very stable and production-ready platform. The OpenStack Foundation has even begun a program of extended support for releases, which would have been otherwise set as end of life. Now, the Foundation is publishing dates for when support will be ending (non-security support) well beyond the release of a new version. Interesting things are happening around OpenStack, and the platform is firmly in the center of many telco-centric programs that make it the virtual infrastructure manager of choice. Furthermore, because more enterprises are now considering using containers in their workloads, they've come to realize that they need an infrastructure platform like OpenStack that will support private cloud workloads on VMs, containers, and bare metal. Because there is a portability to containers and container workloads, OpenStack continues to play a role in a hybrid IT strategy. Although some have said that OpenStack has become boring now that the hype has died down and the platform has proven itself as a stable production cloud software, more projects are created to extend OpenStack almost daily.

In this chapter, we will cover:

- Emerging trends in OpenStack
- Building the roadmap

Emerging trends in OpenStack

One of the most interesting things about the way that OpenStack has evolved over its short history is the vast number of projects that have sprung up around the core set of compute, network, and storage services. As of the Queens release of OpenStack, there were almost 60 projects in the *Big Tent* and about 40 are a part of the release. These projects can be broadly lumped into two categories—those that automate additional infrastructure components and those that manage the installation, configuration, and life cycle of OpenStack itself.

This first set of projects are typically patterned after analogues in Amazon Web Services and provide a fuller *stack* of services to be used in application deployments. The second set of projects contain configuration management code like the Puppet modules we used in earlier chapters to deploy OpenStack and common services and libraries, which are used by the other services. Other services enable operations tools and provide support to those operating OpenStack:

OpenStack Bucket Map

Moving up the stack

Some of the projects that automate additional infrastructure components have become adopted widely enough to be included with commercial vendors' OpenStack distributions. These include projects like Trove, which provides Database as a Service, and Sahara, which provides Data Processing as a Service. These projects leverage the Nova compute service to deploy instances of prepared Glance images that provide end users with higher level resources such as databases over the OpenStack APIs. These resources can then be automated like any other OpenStack resource either through the API or through the Heat orchestration service.

Trove is one of the more mature OpenStack services outside of the core set of original services. Trove allows developers to provision an instance of a given database to support their application without having to design or specify the underlying compute and storage for the database instance. Trove is largely developed by the company Tesora, who offers a certified and supported version of the Trove component for most of the major community and enterprise distributions of OpenStack. At present, Trove supports provisioning a range of relational databases, such as MySQL and PostgreSQL, in addition to NoSQL databases such as MongoDB, Couchbase, Cassandra, and Redis.

Sahara provides big data as a service in OpenStack, largely through the automated deployment of Hadoop clusters. Sahara allows users to create a data processing cluster, define job templates and then execute those jobs on the cluster. Sahara has a large number of integration points to external services like Designate for name resolution and Barbican for certificate management. Jobs can pull data either from external or internal HDFS volumes or from Swift or Manila in OpenStack. Sahara currently supports Apache Hadoop, the Hortonworks Data Platform, Apache Spark, MapR and Cloudera Hadoop as cluster types. Both traditional Hadoop and Spark jobs are supported in the service.

Designate and Barbican are examples of services that provide extended infrastructure automation capabilities to round out application stacks but do not provision instances. Another popular project in this category is Zaqar, which provides Messaging as a Service. Services like these can be extremely attractive to both developers and operators in private cloud environments. Developers no longer have to worry about the details behind the infrastructure components in their application architecture, and operators can rest assured that developers are using these components in standardized ways that are easy to troubleshoot and scale.

New and interesting in Queens is support for vGPUs. This support comes from Nova who has added GPU support to the project. This will allow admins to define flavors that boot VMs which have vGPUs. This feature is extremely important since a lot of scientific workloads are now taking advantage of the high-performance processing GPUs provide. Another new feature in Cinder is the ability to multi-attach a single cinder volume to multiple instances. This is a major improvement that increases resiliency in clustered applications who can share a single data source.

We discussed Zun and Magnum in the containers chapter and how Kuryr and Fuxi fit into orchestration. New in the Queens release is Helm, the package manager for Kubernetes that we also discussed in the Containers chapter.

Building the roadmap

It's an exciting time to be involved in such a rapidly changing project. That excitement should be leveraged by a cloud architect who is looking to gain adoption from application development teams. One way to build interest in the developer community is to continually expand the amount of services that are available to them in the private cloud. As we mentioned earlier, adding capabilities from services like Trove or Designate to the cloud simplifies the work that both developers and operators do. Including developer teams as early-adopters of new features is a great way to build rapport and confidence with them as well.

Introducing new features

A prerequisite for being able to incrementally add new features to an OpenStack deployment is to have a set of test environments available to advance the features through. Cloud engineering teams should have a private environment where they can develop and test new features and another environment where end users can test features before they are rolled out to production cloud environments. Having multiple environments also allows new functionality to bake in, which allows cloud operators the ability to see what the logging, performance, and other impacts of a new feature will be. Instrumentation can also be developed and tested in the lower environments.

New features or capabilities should be introduced incrementally into the platform. In the planning stage, use cases for the capabilities should be defined and test cases should be written. These new features and capabilities should also be tested and deployed in the same manner as code; first in test environments, then into production. As the features are deployed into lower environments, documentation should be updated and test cases for the capabilities should be added to the monitoring regimen. A simple way to test these new capabilities is to write an example Heat orchestration template that exercises them. For example, adding the provisioning of a database to an existing application stack that is already being deployed by Heat. This template can then also be provided to application teams as documentation for the service.

Releasing new versions

One of the most discussed and criticized aspects of OpenStack has always been the major version upgrade procedure. On the upside though, it's also one of the most thoroughly documented and tested aspects of the project. Each major component of OpenStack provides an upgrade path between releases, and most of them support rolling upgrades at this point. Much work has been done to decouple the API versions of the various services to ensure that services can be updated one at a time without downtime. The truth is, though, that it's hard to upgrade an operating private cloud. Users of private clouds expect their workloads to be continuously available. As such, many of the OpenStack adopters that we've worked with have been reluctant to update their clouds once they're in production.

While deploying a release of OpenStack and then running it for a few years is certainly possible (commercial vendors like Red Hat provide support for up to 3 years for a given release of OpenStack), we certainly don't recommend it. Organizations who deployed the Icehouse release of OpenStack and have run it for a couple of years will end up re-engineering much of their configuration management and deployment processes for the Newton release. This work takes a lot of time and effort. Organizations who have stepped through the releases or have deployed a new release every calendar year will have a much smaller amount of change to manage when the new version does come out.

Incremental change has a smaller impact on the developer community as well. As we mentioned earlier, continually improving and updating your Infrastructure as a Service will keep the community engaged and eliminate the need to retrain them every time a new platform is released.

One of the most exciting developments in upgrades has been released in the Queens release. It is called **Fast Forward Upgrades**. It allows users to quickly move through upgrades to get from release N to $N+X$ where, X is greater than 1 and equal to or less than 3, for example, going from Newton to Queens. Originally, this was known as skip-level upgrades; however, you're not actually skipping upgrades. However, this new feature gets OpenStack clouds upgraded as quickly as possible. This is a significant milestone because OpenStack is released on a 6-month release cycle. Most large enterprises are not in sync with this type of rapid change. In the April 2017 User Survey, the majority of respondents were N-2 in their releases and upgrades have been a bi-annual challenge to most operators. Although this feature is just in the beginning stages, it will continue to develop over time and with the introduction of containers into OpenStack infrastructure, the combination of fast forwarding and composable infrastructure should ease the upgrade process tremendously.

Summary

In this book, we walked through the major areas of focus in the emerging practice of a Cloud Architect as it pertains to OpenStack. We showed you some techniques and recommendations to enable you to work with company stakeholders and provide architectural leadership in order to create a holistic design for OpenStack in an enterprise. Successfully designing, deploying, and operating OpenStack clouds requires a wide breadth of knowledge in the fields of compute, network, storage, and software design. It also takes a deep understanding of a company's strategic mission, processes, and success criteria for implementing a private cloud. Successful Cloud Architects leverage the knowledge and practice of subject matter experts in deep technical areas in conjunction with their own knowledge when designing OpenStack clouds. This book was written to provide a framework that an Architect could use to create a successful OpenStack deployment in concert with the rest of an enterprise using modern software development methodologies. Although this book provides a solid foundation for OpenStack architecture, we hope that it has given you tools and confidence to begin your own journey into OpenStack architectural design.

Further reading

Please refer to **OpenStack Projects**: http://governance.openstack.org/reference/projects/.

Other Books You May Enjoy

If you enjoyed this book, you may be interested in these other books by Packt:

OpenStack Cloud Computing Cookbook - Fourth Edition
Kevin Jackson, Cody Bunch, Egle Sigler, James Denton

ISBN: 978-1-78839-876-3

- Understand, install, configure, and manage a complete OpenStack Cloud platform using OpenStack-Ansible
- Configure networks, routers, load balancers, and more with Neutron
- Use Keystone to setup domains, roles, groups and user access
- Learn how to use Swift and setup container access control lists
- Gain hands-on experience and familiarity with Horizon, the OpenStack Dashboard user interface
- Automate complete solutions with our recipes on Heat, the OpenStack Orchestration service as well as using Ansible to orchestrate application workloads
- Follow practical advice and examples to run OpenStack in production

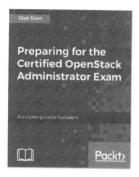

Preparing for the Certified OpenStack Administrator Exam
Matt Dorn

ISBN: 978-1-78728-841-6

- Manage the Keystone identity service by creating and modifying domains, groups, projects, users, roles, services, endpoints, and quotas
- Upload Glance images, launch new Nova instances, and create flavors, key pairs, and snapshots
- Discover Neutron tenant and provider networks, security groups, routers, and floating IPs
- Manage the Cinder block storage service by creating volumes and attaching them to instances
- Create Swift containers and set access control lists to allow read/write access to your objects
- Explore Heat orchestration templates and create, list, and update stacks

Leave a review - let other readers know what you think

Please share your thoughts on this book with others by leaving a review on the site that you bought it from. If you purchased the book from Amazon, please leave us an honest review on this book's Amazon page. This is vital so that other potential readers can see and use your unbiased opinion to make purchasing decisions, we can understand what our customers think about our products, and our authors can see your feedback on the title that they have worked with Packt to create. It will only take a few minutes of your time, but is valuable to other potential customers, our authors, and Packt. Thank you!

Index

56126641R00141

Made in the USA
Columbia, SC
20 April 2019